The deepest desire of every C[...] kids to know and love Christ. *Raising Disciples* addresses parents' core desires and shows them, step-by-step, how to succeed. Dr. Roberts weaves the presence of Christ into a child's normal development in a way that makes growing a child's faith in Christ completely natural.

MEG MEEKER, MD, bestselling author of *Strong Fathers, Strong Daughters*

Raising Disciples provides an easy-to-use template for not only raising disciples but also teaching your church how to raise disciples. Teresa has provided a timely and valuable resource for all Christ followers.

RUSTY GEORGE, lead pastor at Crossroads Christian Church

Teresa Welch Roberts brings clarity on raising children who love Jesus for every parent, teacher, and grandparent. This book offers biblical guidance and practical nurturing, and it doesn't disappoint as a valuable resource for those who want to raise children of faith.

LUCILLE WILLIAMS, author of *The Impossible Kid*

Raising Disciples is a treasure trove of wisdom for parents wanting to guide their children in developing a meaningful relationship with Jesus. Dr. Teresa Roberts has outlined principles for kids at each age level that are both practical and deeply rooted in Scripture. Get this book—it'll help your kids take their next step of faith toward Jesus.

CALEB KALTENBACH, founder of The Messy Grace Group, author of *Messy Grace* and *Messy Truth*, and research pastor at Shepherd Church

At our gigachurch, we are always looking for ways to maximize ROI. That's why we prioritize coaching parents in our kids' ministry. We realize that what Dr. Roberts is advocating for in *Raising Disciples* is, hands down, the single greatest investment of our church to secure the future for God's Kingdom. This is a resource you can't afford to overlook.

MARK E. MOORE, PHD, teaching pastor at Christ's Church of the Valley

Imagine our twelve- and thirteen-year-olds coming of age knowing exactly who they are in Christ, viewing the world through a biblical framework, sorting through questions, and thinking abstractly—all with a trusted faith community beside them. *Raising Disciples* turns this vision into a reality by offering practical guidance to those doing the most fruitful work of the church—child discipleship.

MATT MARKINS, coauthor of *Forming Faith* and CEO of Awana Child Discipleship

Parents who are looking for a compassionate and compelling guide to nurturing their children's faith in Jesus need look no further than *Raising Disciples*. Dr. Teresa Roberts masterfully provides sound biblical principles and relevant stories that will help kids embrace Christ-centered values. I wholeheartedly recommend this book to anyone seeking to lay a powerful spiritual foundation for their children.

DUDLEY RUTHERFORD, senior pastor of Shepherd Church

I've known Dr. Teresa Roberts since she was a grade-schooler. As the weekend youth pastor, I was often hosted in her home, where I observed her humble and godly parents demonstrating intentional discipleship. Teresa's insights are forged not only in tremendous research and academic rigor, for which she is immensely qualified, but also in the lab of real life and practicality lived out by her extraordinary mom and dad, just everyday people who love Jesus and passed that on to their kids. You will be blessed, encouraged, inspired, and informed by this tremendous book.

GENE APPEL, senior pastor of Eastside Christian Church

Why is a college president still teaching children's church after thirty years? I do it because I believe children's ministry is *the* most effective strategy under heaven. Most Americans who decide to follow Jesus do so by age thirteen. In these pages, Dr. Teresa Roberts shows how those first thirteen years are also the most effective *discipleship* opportunity. I know no one better equipped to write about discipling kids than my colleague and friend Teresa, and this book offers wise and clear help to anyone—church leaders, parents, grandparents—who wants to shape children into committed Christ followers. My six kids are grown, but I'll be recommending this book as they now raise my grandchildren.

MATT PROCTOR, president of Ozark Christian College

GUIDING YOUR KIDS

INTO A FAITH

OF THEIR OWN

Raising Disciples

TERESA ROBERTS

A NavPress resource published in alliance with Tyndale House Publishers

NavPress.com

Raising Disciples: Guiding Your Kids into a Faith of Their Own

Copyright © 2024 by Teresa Roberts. All rights reserved.

A NavPress resource published in alliance with Tyndale House Publishers

NavPress and the NavPress logo are registered trademarks of NavPress, The Navigators, Colorado Springs, CO. *Tyndale* is a registered trademark of Tyndale House Ministries. Absence of ® in connection with marks of NavPress or other parties does not indicate an absence of registration of those marks.

The Team:
David Zimmerman, Publisher; Caitlyn Carlson, Acquisitions Editor; Deborah Sáenz Gonzalez, Developmental Editor; Elizabeth Schroll, Copyeditor; Olivia Eldredge, Operations Manager; Sarah Susan Richardson, Designer

Cover illustration of road map by Sarah Susan Richardson. Copyright © 2024 by NavPress/The Navigators. All rights reserved.

Author photo copyright © 2023 by Mark Nevenschwander. All rights reserved.

Published in association with literary agent Don Gates of The Gates Group, the-gates -group.com

Some of the anecdotal illustrations in this book are true to life and are included with the permission of the persons involved. All other illustrations are composites of real situations, and any resemblance to people living or dead is purely coincidental.

For information about special discounts for bulk purchases, please contact Tyndale House Publishers at csresponse@tyndale.com, or call 1-855-277-9400.

ISBN 978-1-64158-863-8

Printed in the United States of America

30 29 28 27 26 25 24
7   6   5   4   3   2   1

Contents

To Lyle and Judy Welch,
who raised me to be a disciple of Jesus

Preface

My earliest memory is of a water tower.

Yes, you read that correctly—a water tower.

The first four years of my life were spent in Newark, Ohio. I can't remember the two-story white house in which we lived. Pictures don't jog memories of my bedroom or the family room where I played. The one thing I clearly remember from that time in my life—some forty-five years later—is a water tower, or perhaps more specifically, what that water tower signified.

Passing by that water tower meant we were driving to church. I would see it out the window from my car seat as we drove and know exactly where we were going. Accompanying that memory are the feelings I had when I spotted that water tower—excitement, joy, happiness. We were going to church; it was my favorite place to be.

That water tower is the first in a series of symbols of my discipleship journey. It signifies the priority my parents placed on Christ. It indicates their commitment to participating in a local church community. It symbolizes that from my infancy, God has been the central character in my story.

The result of my parents' placing Christ and the church at the center of our family was that a college math professor and a bank accountant raised three children to be disciples. My younger brothers and I were typical kids who grew up in a small, Midwestern college town. We went to public schools, participated in sports and music, and did well academically. We also had sibling squabbles and had our actions and attitudes corrected from time to time. But because our parents raised us to be disciples, we each made a commitment to Christ in childhood, grew in our walk with Jesus through our teenage years, answered the call to vocational Christian service, graduated from Bible college, and are now discipling others in our families and ministries.

Our parents didn't raise perfect kids. They didn't intend to raise us to enter vocational ministry. What they did was put Christ at the center of our family and guide us on a journey with Christ.

This journey included my parents placing us in the middle of a Christian community. This was more than attending church on Sunday mornings. Our weekly schedule and annual calendar centered around participation in our church community. We lived hours away from my grandparents and extended family, but because of the church, I had "adopted" grandfathers, grandmothers, aunts, and uncles. I was discipled by and through this community.

Twenty years after passing that water tower week after week, I was called to serve as the children's minister at a church located about an hour away. For more than twenty-five years I have served the church—first as a children's minister and currently as a Bible college professor and a children's ministry volunteer. I have loved participating in the discipleship of thousands of children.

Over the course of years of children's discipleship, I have learned one very clear lesson: I can spend hours preparing lessons, writing curriculum, training volunteers, and planning events, but ultimately the discipleship of children centers on the home. Moms, dads, stepparents, foster parents, and other caregivers are the primary influencers in raising a child to be a disciple.

But God has not left parents to do this work alone. He has created us for community and placed us in the family of God. That means every person who interacts with a child—children's ministers, grandparents, small-group leaders and volunteers, aunts and uncles, family friends, and other ministry staff members—has a part to play in raising disciples.

This book is written for everyone who desires to partner with God in the discipleship of children. My desire is to help you engage children by empowering them to become the followers of Christ God has created them to be. By guiding them along the discipleship map introduced within these pages, you can direct each one you encounter toward developing a relationship with God and their identity in Christ.

CHAPTER 1

Becoming like Christ

The first thirteen years of life are the most important years for discipleship.[1]

As I write this sentence, I can hear my friends who work with teenagers raise objections to this statement as they describe their work with middle school and high school students. I can see on my office shelves several books about discipleship of adults. In my current work, I'm surrounded by college students—these emerging adults—and I come alongside students as their belief in Christ deepens in those four years. Discipleship is a lifelong process, and each stage of that process is important.

But I will argue that the first thirteen years of life are the most important in this lifelong process of discipleship. No other time between birth and death provides as many opportunities to shape how individuals perceive themselves, others, and the world. This is by God's design.

While we can witness the rapid growth of a child's physical body,[2] what is happening in their mind is even more miraculous and formational. In fact, it is during these first thirteen years of life that humans develop cognitive skills,[3] social competencies,[4] and moral commitments[5] at a rate that exceeds any other time of life.[6]

By the time a child reaches adolescence, she will have a cognitive framework—a mindset—that organizes her world into clear categories. This framework begins with concrete thinking: understanding the world through her senses and direct experiences. By age thirteen, she will mature beyond concrete thinking to abstract thought through the conceptualizing of ideas, critical reasoning, and understanding hypothetical scenarios. During childhood, her social world shifts from being self-centered toward being others-centered (and to a desire to be valued by others). By age thirteen, she can identify right from wrong, describe her basic beliefs, and make decisions based on what she values most. Many of the choices we make, passions we pursue, and perspectives we articulate as adults can be traced back to what we learned and believed in childhood.[7]

In other words, the first thirteen years of life are the most active in our development as humans and therefore in our development as followers of Jesus.

This process of biological, cognitive, social, and moral maturation is commonly labeled *childhood development*. But

I suggest that we could also label the process of maturation during childhood in this way: *discipleship.*

Defining *Discipleship*

Christians often associate the term *discipleship* with the process of becoming more like Jesus, but by its most basic definition, discipleship is *the process by which a student becomes more like the person or subject he or she is following.*

Every child is in the process of discipleship. The question is *What is discipling them?*

Consider a day in the life of your child. Who are the people she is following—peers, teachers, celebrities, coaches? How much time does he spend at athletic practices or watching sports on television? Who is teaching her to dance en pointe, dismount from the balance beam, or play the piano? How much emphasis is being placed on homework and academic achievement? What grabs his attention on YouTube or TV? How much time is she spending playing video games or reading books? Children are being discipled through academics, athletics, extracurricular activities, relationships, and entertainment. Every child is in the process of discipleship, whether intentionally begun or not. If her discipleship is focused primarily on these types of activities, consider the natural result. She might be an excellent athlete, academically strong, or socially active—but is she following Jesus?

Now consider the amount of time your child spends in Christ-centered activities in a day. How much time does he spend reading the Bible, singing songs about God, or in prayer? Is she participating in a Christian community to learn about faith, worship God, and be in fellowship with other believers? Does your family gather for meals to share about your day or have Christ-centered conversations regularly? Does he walk or hike trails to appreciate the beauty of God's creation? How often do you take advantage of everyday moments to point her to Jesus?

Hear me well. I'm not suggesting that playing Little League, taking piano lessons, or focusing on academics is bad. Not at all. Children need a variety of activities and relationships to grow into well-rounded, healthy adults.[8] Under the right circumstances, almost every experience can come under the lordship of Christ and be part of the process of discipleship in Christ. I'm also not saying that parents should place their children inside a Christ-centered bubble and not allow them to interact with anything that isn't explicitly "of God." Instead, I suggest regularly evaluating a day in the life of our children to consider what we are emphasizing and the choices we are helping them make.

We need to recognize that from infancy children are being discipled. At the same time children are growing taller, learning vocabulary words, developing social skills, and starting to understand themselves and others, they are developing their beliefs about God, God's Word, and God's work in their lives and the world. In the same way we teach them to read, practice a sport with them, and help them develop good manners, we should actively and intentionally place our children on a discipleship journey toward Christ. We can't just expect children to arrive at the destination of belief in God; we need to guide them along the path. We need to ask this question on a regular basis: Are they following Jesus and becoming increasingly more like Him?

One of the joys I've had as a children's minister is observing those I identify as "my kids" grow and mature into young adults. I've had the honor of attending their weddings, holding their children, and even teaching some of them in college. What I've consistently witnessed as "my kids" mature into adulthood is directly connected to the observations I made about them during their childhood. These young men and women are in many ways just older—and taller—versions of the children I discipled. Much of their personalities, habits, and interests remain the same—just more mature and, sometimes, more intense.

Proverbs 22:6 encourages us to "start children off on the way they should go, and even when they are old they will not turn from it." This proverb is not a promise that every child will remain in Christ—a child's disposition and life events can work contrary to the gospel. But research indicates that adults who follow Jesus most likely made a commitment to Him in childhood.[9]

Becoming more like Christ—engaging in lifelong discipleship—is the expectation of every follower of Jesus. Christian publishers regularly release books on discipleship topics to help guide adults in their Christian maturity. Middle school and high school ministries include discipleship groups as part of their weekly programs. Some churches designate a ministry staff member to focus on discipleship. When discipleship discussions take place, however, they often focus on adolescents and adults rather than children.

Why?

Perhaps it's because Jesus chose twelve young men—teenagers and young adults—as disciples during His ministry. Maybe it's because there are few examples of the discipleship of children in Scripture, so it's difficult to identify a pattern to follow. But I believe the most common reason is that the ability of children to be discipled is underestimated due to the immaturity of their thinking and choices. Many adults assume it is better to wait until a child's cognitive abilities have matured before beginning the process of discipleship rather than to see the opportunities for effective discipleship that childhood presents.

If you weren't already convinced that children can be discipled and that the first thirteen years of life are *the* most important for discipleship, remember this: Jesus believed childhood was so important that He lived it. The God of all creation came to earth in the person of Jesus not as a twelve-year-old or a thirty-year-old but as an infant.

Consider for a moment that Jesus experienced every stage of childhood. He learned to sit up, crawl, stand, and walk. He learned how to speak and the meaning of words. He played with friends, completed chores, and grew up alongside other children. Between the time Jesus was dedicated at the Temple at forty days old (Luke 2:22) and when He attended the Festival of the Passover at twelve years old (Luke 2:42), Scripture records that Jesus "grew and became strong; he was filled with wisdom, and the grace of God was on him" (Luke 2:40). In other words, Jesus experienced physical, cognitive, social, and spiritual growth firsthand in those early years of life on earth.

It remains a mystery what Scripture means when it says that Jesus

> made himself nothing
>> by taking the very nature of a servant,
>> being made in human likeness.
>
> PHILIPPIANS 2:7

We do not know whether the wisdom of the universe was in the mind of the infant wrapped in swaddling clothes and lying in a manger (Luke 2:7). But we should not underestimate the importance of Jesus living childhood so that He might empathize with the whole of life's experiences.

In accordance with Jewish tradition, Jesus attended the Festival of the Passover at age twelve. This year was labeled the "age of discernment" in preparation for the rite of passage into adolescence at age thirteen, when Jewish males were expected to bear the weight of God's law.[10] The Gospel of Luke records that Jesus remained in Jerusalem after the Festival of the Passover. Though He worried Mary and Joseph when they discovered that Jesus was absent from the group returning to their home in Nazareth of Galilee (Luke 2:48),

He demonstrated, with words and actions, awareness of His identity and purpose. Jesus asked His parents, "Didn't you know I had to be in my Father's house?" (Luke 2:49), which can also be translated as ". . . about my Father's business?"[11]

According to the psychosocial development research of Erik Erikson, it is around age twelve that children enter a stage of self-awareness and social development when they are faced with finding out who they are, what they are about, and where they are going in life.[12] Therefore, just like Jesus, by the time a child reaches adolescence, they can believe that they are a child of God whose purpose is to live in the presence of God and be about their Father's business. They'll be more likely to believe this truth if we raise them as disciples.

The Goal for *Raising Disciples*

The first thirteen years of life are the most important for discipleship . . . so what can we do?

Though the Bible does not provide us with step-by-step instructions for raising children to be disciples, it does provide commands to parents and examples of discipleship that can be helpful and instructive. Though not all children develop biologically, cognitively, socially, and morally in the same way, we can rely on research that helps us understand the stages of childhood development that God designed. And though each child's journey with Christ will be unique based on a variety of factors, there is a clear goal for their discipleship journey, and there are some general directions we can guide them along on their journey.

Chapter 2 provides a discipleship map to use in guiding children in a life of discipleship from infancy to adolescence. Built on a biblical description for the process of discipleship, this map integrates information from childhood development to provide directions for spiritual growth. The goal of these steps in a child's discipleship journey is that they will never know a life outside of Christ. Instead, their faith will be nurtured from infancy toward a relationship with God that flourishes and matures throughout their life.

After the discipleship map is introduced, subsequent chapters provide ideas for each stage in raising a disciple. These chapters provide guidance on how to teach children to become students of the Bible, build a vocabulary of faith, and develop spiritual practices to develop an identity in Christ and a relationship with God. At the conclusion of the book, appendix D ("Age-Level Discipleship") contains information from each chapter organized by age group as a reference in guiding a child into a faith of their own.

Though this book is oriented toward parents and primary caregivers of children, the discipleship map and the additional information provided is helpful for anyone who is participating in the discipleship of a child. So whether you are a children's ministry leader or volunteer, a grandparent or a godparent, or an amazing aunt or uncle, this resource is for you, too. It takes the whole family of God to raise a disciple. In appendices A and B, you'll find additional questions for reflection and resources helpful for anyone who participates in the discipleship of kids.

Let's link arms to guide the children in our lives along this pathway toward faith and commitment to Christ.

God Makes Things Grow

From the very beginning, I want to acknowledge that not every child is born into a Christian family, nor does every child have the ability or opportunity to grow in ideal circumstances. Whether a child has barriers to their growth or experiences trauma that impacts their development, not all children will progress in their discipleship in the same way. I encourage you to disciple every child, wherever they are along this path, in a way unique to their circumstances and experiences. Recognize potential barriers to their growth, but also identify the opportunities.

A good reminder is that though we can lead, train, encourage, and empower kids in their discipleship, God is the One who makes things grow (1 Corinthians 3:6-9). God knows each child and their location along the discipleship map. May we rest in the knowledge that God is at work in our lives as we become more like Christ and in the lives of the children we are raising to follow Him.

TYING IT ALL TOGETHER

As Jesus' earthly ministry was coming to its conclusion, He traveled with the twelve disciples through towns where He would heal the sick and teach the crowds the Good News of the Kingdom of God. His teachings challenged the religious leaders, but they also challenged His followers in their understanding of His message. And as they traveled, people desired to be near this miracle-working teacher.

> People were also bringing babies to Jesus for him to place his hands on them. When the disciples saw this, they rebuked them. But Jesus called the children to him and said, "Let the little children come to me, and do not hinder them, for the kingdom of God belongs to such as these. Truly I tell you, anyone who will not receive the kingdom of God like a little child will never enter it."
> LUKE 18:15-17

Notice in this encounter what Jesus did and did not do.

Jesus did not summon the parents to come. Jesus summoned children. Jesus did not say that once a child matures they become a disciple. Jesus said that children are in the Kingdom of God *now*. Jesus did not keep children at arm's length. Jesus rebuked the disciples and admonished everyone not to hinder children. Jesus did not say that the disciples or religious leaders were the example to follow. Instead, Jesus said that children are our example of how to receive the Kingdom.

PUTTING IT INTO PRACTICE
Questions for Reflection

1. Create a chart or map of your family's weekly schedule. List the regular activities for each family member from the past few months.

2. Review the chart and answer the following question: What or who is discipling your child?

3. Reflect on your own childhood and how you were discipled during the first thirteen years of your life. In what ways do you want your child's discipleship to be similar? Different?

4. How does your childhood experience of discipleship influence the way you're discipling children?

CHAPTER 2

The Discipleship Map

When I was a child, a couple of times a year my family would journey from our home in central Illinois to visit my grandmother in southern Minnesota. Because we traveled that path so frequently, I knew the six-hour route very well. I knew when we would cross the Mississippi River and pass the Quaker Oats sign—which was important when you were searching for that elusive *Q* in the alphabet game. I knew how many hours in the car were left when we passed through certain towns or that our trip would be extended when we turned down the road that led to my aunt and uncle's farm. Even today, I can point out the location where our family van exceeded the speed limit early one Thanksgiving morning and my dad received his first traffic ticket.

During those trips I learned how to read a state road map. I still carry an old-school atlas with me in the car, just in case. But today we can open an app on our phones or on the car dashboard to provide us with cues for our travels. The GPS tells us when to exit, merge with traffic, and change lanes. It can provide alternate routes based on traffic, suggest the closest coffee shop, or exclaim "Recalculating route!" when you miss your turn.

But what's the one thing necessary for a GPS system to function as it has been designed?

A destination.

When it comes to raising disciples, we should set our eyes on the destination.

I believe that one of the reasons parents and caregivers struggle to disciple children well is that we haven't clearly identified the destination for their discipleship and the directions that guide them toward that goal.

How would you describe a child who is entering adolescence as an active disciple? Would you choose words that describe their character: *loving, joyful, obedient, self-controlled*? Or would you choose words that describe behaviors: *reads the Bible daily, asks spiritual questions, worships God*? Perhaps you would choose words that describe their depth of knowledge and understanding about God and His Word.

Public and private education systems have stated objectives when it comes to student expectations. Lists of student learning outcomes articulate the goals for students at the conclusion of each grade level. Each child is unique and develops at their own rate, so there are those who will exceed the expectations and others who will struggle. But teachers begin each year knowing the goals and guiding students along the path toward achievement. Like a GPS, they might have to find alternative paths for some or help others get turned back around, but with a clear goal and markers on the way, teachers are able to guide their young disciples.

This is what we've been missing in our homes and churches—a discipleship map that states the goal for raising disciples and provides directions toward that goal.

In some Christian traditions, the goal for children has been a public confession of Christ; in others, submission through the act of baptism. In yet other traditions, it has been completion of confirmation classes. Regardless of our traditions, our goal for raising disciples should be the same as the goal for all disciples: to become more and more like Christ every day.

For three years, Jesus taught the crowds, His enemies, and political leaders, but most often, He was teaching twelve ordinary men from various backgrounds, vocations, and experiences. When He chose the Twelve, He had a goal in mind. Jesus knew that at the conclusion of His earthly ministry He would redeem the world through His death, return to God the Father, and equip His followers with the Holy Spirit to disciple others. He needed a core group of leaders who would follow Him daily (Luke 9:23), continuing His mission "to seek and to save the lost" (Luke 19:10) and to "make disciples of all nations" (Matthew 28:19).

As Jesus prepared to leave the Twelve to continue His mission, He met with them to give them some final encouragements and admonitions. Woven through Jesus' conversation in the upper room (John 13–17), we find descriptions of what it means to become like Christ—follow His example (John 13:14-15), love others (John 13:34), believe in God (John 14:1), keep God's commands (John 14:15), and remain in Christ (John 15:4). These descriptors provide some direction toward the goal for all disciples.

With the destination of becoming like Christ as our goal, we can utilize childhood development information from the fields of social science, learning theory, and psychology to create a map for discipleship from infancy to adolescence.[1] Beginning at birth, there are seven directional discipleship markers—approximately one for every two years of life—that parallel the biological, cognitive, social, and moral development of children. Just as Jesus discipled the Twelve from spiritual infancy to spiritual maturity, we can use this map to raise disciples who become increasingly more like Christ.

THE DISCIPLESHIP MAP

Champion God's Calling
(11-12 years)

Reinforce God's Commands
(9-10 years)

Teach God's Truth
(7-8 years)

Engage God's Community
(5-6 years)

Share God's Story
(3-4 years)

Demonstrate God's Love
(1-2 years)

Establish God's Foundation
(0-12 months)

Note: For more on this, see appendix C.

Establish God's Foundation: Ages 0–12 Months (Infants)

A little bundle of joy held in a mother's arms. A newborn being rocked by a caring nursery worker. The silly faces of a father that elicit those first giggles . . .

DEVELOPMENT OF INFANTS *(Ages 0–12 Months)*

Discipleship Direction: Establish God's Foundation

Infants develop a sense of trust by forming a secure attachment with their caregivers, built upon constant care and genuine concern. Help establish an infant's attachment to God by laying this foundation of trust.

Cognitive and Behavioral Development	Emotional, Social, and Moral Development
• learn large motor skills (rolling over, crawling, walking) • mimic the facial expressions of others • look at self in a mirror • respond to their name • begin to say simple words • are egocentric (do not comprehend a world that exists outside themselves)	• recognize familiar faces • identify those who are unfamiliar as strangers • learn appropriate trust and distrust • thrive in a safe, consistent, and loving space • learn how to react to actions and express emotions • sense the emotions of their caregivers and the mood in their environment

Our belief in God is being formed before we begin to understand sights or sounds. The feelings a child develops from their very first moments—of safety and caring and affection—set the direction for discipleship.[2] It begins with trust, the belief that someone or something is reliable. Before a child can believe in God, obey His Word, and make a lifelong commitment to Him, he must trust that God exists and that His Word is true. Trust is foundational for developing relationships with others, most importantly with God. Therefore, the first direction on the discipleship map is to establish a foundation of trust rooted in God's character.

Beginning from early moments in the mother's womb, a child learns how—and whom—to trust. Infants learn to trust when they cry and someone provides for their needs. Trust is learned through consistent people, constant care, and a safe, secure environment. A newborn learns he can trust his parents, even when he is not in the same physical space as them—such as in a church nursery with another caregiver or while sleeping in an adjacent room at home. When his parents return after an appropriate length of time, he learns the reassurance of a trusting relationship. The process of developing "object permanence" has been documented in psychology circles and serves as an illustration for how an infant creates a secure attachment with his primary caregivers.[3]

As an infant learns to trust the people she can see and interact with, this places her on a path to trust in a God who is unseen and beyond understanding. When a parent or adult is consistent and reliable through their interactions with an infant, she will trust in what they say as well as what they do. If a trusted adult points a child toward God, this helps her build a secure attachment with the One who is worthy of our trust.

During the first twelve months of life, a child begins to recognize oft-repeated words from those he trusts. Teach him the words *God*, *Jesus*, and *Bible*. These words become foundational for his faith. Though we may never fully understand the impact of our words and actions on the faith development of infants, we should not take these first months of learning for granted. It's never too early to help children begin their discipleship by helping them build a secure, trusting attachment to God.

Demonstrate God's Love: Ages 1-2 Years (Toddlers)

She toddles across the room with her arms open wide to give her daddy a big hug. He squeezes his older sister's neck and plants a big kiss on her cheek. He snuggles into mom's arms at night as she reads him a bedtime story . . .

DEVELOPMENT OF TODDLERS *(Ages 1–2 Years)*

Discipleship Direction: Demonstrate God's Love

Toddlers perceive love through expressions such as hugs and kisses as well as through hearing the words "I love you." Demonstrate love through your words and actions. Tell them that God loves them too.

Cognitive and Behavioral Development	Emotional, Social, and Moral Development
• master large motor skills through constant movement • practice fine motor skills • learn through their five senses and repeated activities • learn speech through repetition of hearing and saying words • begin to understand the meaning of words that are frequently repeated	• imitate the actions of others • need a safe environment where they feel secure and loved • are appropriately fearful of strangers until familiarity is established • play alongside rather than with other children and learn appropriate behaviors • have a self-centered view of the world

The word *love* encompasses so much in our lives and in our faith. Love is used to describe emotions and feelings. It is used to describe actions. Love describes the nature of God (1 John 4:8) and His affection for us (1 John 4:9-10). Love describes God's desire for humans to have relationships with Him and with one another (Matthew 22:35-40).

Though the abstract concept of love won't be fully understood until adulthood, experiences with love happen very early in life. Building upon a foundation of trust, when caregivers demonstrate God's love, they place a child firmly on a path toward the One who loves us like no other.

A child's understanding of love at this stage is based on concrete expressions, such as hugs and kisses. As toddlers, children also begin to make connections between the actions of love and those who love them. Encourage children in their discipleship by surrounding them with unconditional love. This continues the process for a child to develop a secure attachment to God through a belief in God's unconditional love for them.

Learning to say basic vocabulary words by repetition is key for the growth of a toddler. One of the earliest phrases a child hears repeatedly is "Mama loves you" or "Dada loves you." Add to this "God loves you." As we teach her to say phrases like "I love Sissy" or "I love Grandpa," we can also help her begin to express her affection for God. Open Bible storybooks with these youngest learners, and when you do, remind them that these stories are about how much God loves us.

Share God's Story: Ages 3-4 Years (Preschoolers)

A song comes on the radio and she sings along, waving her arms like in the video she has watched on repeat. He follows his older cousin around the house, imitating his actions and repeating the words he's using. She uses her pint-size rake to scoop leaves at Daddy's side, just as he's doing with his much bigger rake . . .

DEVELOPMENT OF PRESCHOOLERS *(Ages 3-4 Years)*

Discipleship Direction: Share God's Story
Preschoolers shape their understanding of the world through the stories they hear, see, and experience. Involve them in reading the stories of the Bible and engage them in the rituals of worship, prayer, and service.

Cognitive and Behavioral Development	Emotional, Social, and Moral Development
• are extremely active with bursts of energy • have a short attention span (three to five minutes per activity) • have a rapidly growing vocabulary; use words appropriately without fully understanding their meaning • demonstrate curiosity through asking "Why?" repeatedly • can follow directions, but only one at a time • do not differentiate between make-believe and reality • learn about the world through concrete experiences	• begin to understand right and wrong through behavior and correction • imitate the actions and words of those around them • transition from playing alone to playing with others • learn to share and to cooperate with others through taking turns • act according to emotions and feelings • need a loving environment with consistent routines and boundaries

Children soak up everything they're experiencing at ages three and four—every story they hear, image they see, and song they listen to. Though it will be a few years before they make meaning from these experiences, the events of these years make a lasting impression. Share the stories of God with preschoolers to give context to the trust and love that has been encouraged as they continue along the discipleship map.

Our knowledge of God comes to us primarily through stories. Though Scripture also includes songs, commands, and encouragements, much of the content of the Bible is in the form of story. From the stories of Old Testament characters found in the books of the Law to the stories of the kings and prophets to the story of Jesus in the Gospels and the church in Acts, Scripture shows us the character of God through stories. Our faith in God grows as we become increasingly aware of Him through the stories of His people.

At ages three and four, children build their understanding of themselves and the world through stories: the stories they read at bedtime, the stories they watch on screens, and the stories they hear from adults. At this stage of their lives, a child believes every story he hears is true. He combines the worlds of make-believe and reality. It's the perfect age to help him envision Old Testament characters like Joseph, Ruth, and Daniel. He can imagine himself walking alongside Jesus as He teaches a crowd and performs miracles.

During the preschool years, a child's world expands exponentially as she learns and uses new vocabulary. It starts with words that directly relate to her concrete world (*ball, cat, sister*), activities (*share, try, color*), and emotions (*mad, happy, hurt*). Introducing her to the words of faith through the stories she hears begins to develop her faith vocabulary. Children desire to use these words correctly, even as they are still developing their understanding of the meaning of the words.

At this age, children become aware of themselves, of others, and of events and activities. They begin building an understanding of their own story through the rituals of their days and weeks. Daily morning, mealtime, and bedtime rituals, along with weekly rituals with a church community, help preschoolers know what is valuable and important. Though it will be some time before they fully understand their experiences, their perspective of themselves, others, and the world is built on the things in which preschoolers participate regularly.

Engage God's Community: Ages 5–6 Years (Kindergartners)

She jumps into the car at the end of the school day and hands her mom the picture she colored in class. He places his bedtime reading book on his lap and carefully sounds out the unknown word, looking for affirmation from his dad. She and her friends mimic being teenagers during recess . . .

DEVELOPMENT OF KINDERGARTNERS *(Ages 5-6 Years)*

Discipleship Direction: Engage God's Community

Kindergartners actively engage in learning through school and various activities. Encourage their involvement in exploring Bible stories and sharing prayers. Create an environment where they are comfortable asking questions and sharing their thoughts and opinions.

Cognitive and Behavioral Development	Emotional, Social, and Moral Development
• are very active as they grow in their large and fine motor skills • have a growing attention span as they establish a consistent routine • mix their imagination and reality • have a growing vocabulary with a desire to understand new words as they learn to read	• enjoy playing with other children • begin to relate to adults beyond their parents (teachers, coaches, family friends) • develop a sense of right and wrong based on rules and consequences • begin to see themselves as separate from others • are eager to please adults and desire praise for doing things well • need consistent and loving boundaries and Christlike behavior modeled • observe the behaviors of others and recognize inconsistency

As a child begins formal schooling, usually around age five or six, her world expands quickly. She has new adults teaching her and more children her age with whom to interact. Immerse her in a Christian community as part of this ever-widening world of influence. Discipleship picks up speed as she becomes active in her learning and participates in a wide variety of activities.

It is within a community of faith—at home and church—where the stories, songs, and prayers of earlier years begin to have significance. Rather than playing *alongside* others, he now plays *with* others. The same thing happens in his participation in the activities of faith. As a preschooler, he sang songs or said prayers by echoing adults and others around him. At age five or six, a child begins to proactively participate in the regular rhythms and practices of faith. He may ask to sing a song or hear a story because it has meaning for him. He can choose his own words for prayers rather than repeating the words given to him by others. These rituals will become more important in his faith formation as he actively participates in them.

Children hear thousands of sounds a day. But there is a difference between hearing and listening. Listening is actively participating with what we're hearing. It means understanding a sound and reacting appropriately to it. As she begins to understand the meaning behind the words she is learning, a child can respond appropriately. Kindergartners can learn to make good choices by listening to God's commands and practicing the appropriate responses over and over.

At this age a child becomes an active participant in their own discipleship. In the previous stages children rely on the regular guidance of adults, but as a child learns skills to become more independent, he can make choices on his path toward Jesus.

Teach God's Truth: Ages 7–8 Years (1st and 2nd Graders)

He runs into the house waving the paper with the word *Perfect* written across the top, knocking his little sister aside in his haste. He looks at his grandpa, who is telling him a story about working on the farm, and asks, "Are you making that up?" She leaps off the edge of the pool for a front flip, heedless of how deep or shallow the water is . . .

DEVELOPMENT OF 1ST AND 2ND GRADERS *(Ages 7–8 Years)*

Discipleship Direction: Teach God's Truth

First and second graders grasp the significance of God's stories by acknowledging the reality of God and the truth of God's Word. Encourage them to use their growing vocabulary of faith. Empower them to make decisions to follow Christ and obey God's commands.

Cognitive and Behavioral Development	Emotional, Social, and Moral Development
• are active, talkative, imaginative, and eager to learn new information • have a continually expanding vocabulary as they learn to read and write • have a growing understanding of the world through concrete experiences • begin to separate their understanding of what is real and what is make-believe	• like to play with others and be involved in groups • seek attention from teachers and other adults; imitate their behaviors • develop an understanding of and attitude toward self and others • are emotionally immature; act based on emotions • develop a sense of right and wrong based on consequences • need patient, caring adults who listen to questions and provide a safe environment

Curiosity and *inconsistency* are two words that describe these years of a child's life. The knowledge he is acquiring shapes his understanding of the world as he begins to understand what is true and false. He will often stumble as he tries to do something right and good because of his impulsivity. But as his understanding of God and God's Word moves him along the discipleship map, his obedience to God's commands will become more consistent. Provide direction by teaching him God's truth found in the stories he has learned.

The Word of God was given to us so that we might know God and walk in His ways (Psalm 119:105; 2 Timothy 3:16-17). The stories children have heard since infancy become the stories that shape their thoughts and actions as they mature during middle childhood. Children begin to connect the stories they can recall with events in their lives. These stories guide them in determining right from wrong and making good choices.

Children ages seven to eight are primarily concrete thinkers. Their understanding is based on what they learn through their senses and experiences rather than through ideas, logic, or reason. During these formative years, children begin to grow beyond concrete thinking by first separating their experiences into two categories: make-believe and reality. And though some might want to hold on to that imaginary friend a little longer, most begin to identify what they accept as true and real. As children begin to learn how to solve simple math problems, discover countries on a globe, and hear about events in history, they begin to collect pieces of information and knowledge that will lead to an understanding of themselves and their world over time. As children learn a variety of facts that will become the foundation of their knowledge of the world, they can be taught about the truth of Scripture and the reality of God.

Taking captive teachable moments is key for this age group! Help a child identify her current experience using the vocabulary she has at hand, then tie that into a Christ-centered perspective. (More on teachable moments in chapter 4.)

During these first years of elementary school, a child begins to develop an understanding of right and wrong as his moral compass begins to be calibrated. He begins to develop an awareness that there is a reason for the rules established in his home, school, and church. Help him by connecting his obedience to these rules with God's commands to obey. Point out how his disobedience not only results in consequences but also harms his relationships. At this age, he will be able to articulate that choosing to disobey is a sin and will begin to feel the pangs of guilt that result from his disobedience.

As a child continues in her discipleship, first and second grade are key for helping her realize the path she has been set on toward Christ. Encourage her to take her own steps along this journey by supporting her desires to learn on her own and providing directions to help her stay on the path.

Reinforce God's Commands: Ages 9–10 Years (3rd and 4th Graders)

Strewn across her bedroom floor are soccer cleats, a dance costume, and art supplies as she sits on her bed practicing for the upcoming spelling bee. He sits on the sideline, frustrated that he can't play every minute of the game, especially since his coach tells him he's the best player on the team. She beams proudly when her teacher acknowledges her correct answer, trying to ignore the snickering of the boy sitting behind her . . .

DEVELOPMENT OF 3RD AND 4TH GRADERS *(Ages 9–10 Years)*

Discipleship Direction: Reinforce God's Commands

Third and fourth graders can connect the stories about God to their thoughts about God as they actively participate in the formation of their own beliefs. Guide them toward repentance as they are convicted about their sins and aware of their feelings of guilt. Lead them to accept God's forgiveness and grace.

Cognitive and Behavioral Development	Emotional, Social, and Moral Development
• learn through active engagement in concrete experiences	• desire to be recognized by adults and assist them in their work
• begin to demonstrate strength in certain skills and pursue opportunities related to their strengths	• want to be accepted and belong to a group of peers, usually of the same gender
• develop speed and accuracy in skills through repetition	• believe what is right and wrong is based on adherence to rules or what is fair
• are frustrated by activities that are beyond their abilities	• become less dependent upon their parents and other adults
• begin to understand abstract concepts but are more comfortable with concrete experiences, stories, or examples	• are unable to regulate emotions (which may be expressed in anger or teasing)
• are able to understand past, present, and future and can place events in order	• need a patient, caring adult who encourages their skills and provides assistance in areas that are beyond their ability level
• make connections between information they are learning and their own experience	

These years of discovery build on children's knowledge base as information is categorized, vocabulary holds meaning, and skills are honed. In third and fourth grade a child's conscience grows louder as she becomes aware of her inner voice. As she continues along her journey of discipleship, her belief in God's power and presence can lead her to hear God's voice of conviction and forgiveness. Reinforce God's commands by reminding her of what she's learned and helping her apply it in her life.

It's one thing to say something aloud and quite another to *believe* what's being said. A third or fourth grader can repeat information, recall definitions of words, and share aloud what he's been taught. But at this age, a child begins to challenge what he has learned. He will begin to see conflicts between his thoughts and ideas and those of others. He recognizes inconsistencies. He has separated reality from fantasy and begins to place things into a framework for his beliefs. As he says things aloud, he wrestles with whether he believes those things are true. A caregiver helping a child identify their current experience using the vocabulary they have at hand and then tying that into a Christ-centered perspective should be an everyday occurrence.

As a child understands that something is true and therefore reliable, this leads her to belief. During this period, she may have a plethora of questions as to how she can believe in a God she cannot see. Take every opportunity to create a space for her to ask questions and be heard. It's tempting to "rescue" your child during this age by telling her the answers, but instead she needs guidance toward discovering the answers. This helps her build confidence in using the faith vocabulary she's learning and making connections between Scripture and her life.

This is an opportune time for you to share your story of discipleship with your child. Have grandparents, mentors, and friends share their stories as well. When children hear the stories of adults who have placed their trust in God, this helps them see the story of God at work in the lives of those they know and trust. Be honest about the good times and the hard times. Describe how Jesus makes a difference in your everyday life.

In these years a child begins to differentiate himself from others. He begins to learn that he has skills, gifts, and abilities that are different from those of others. This can lead to a lot of disappointment as he discovers that he can't do some things his friends can or may not have the same opportunities others have. His friend group and extracurricular activities fall in line with these discoveries. He is becoming independent while simultaneously needing help from you and other adults. He fiercely wants to be successful at things yet gets easily frustrated when things don't go well and he "can't do it"—often giving up altogether. He needs tasks that are challenging but can be accomplished.

The natural progression of a child's understanding of truth and that which is right leads to her ability to articulate what she believes about herself, about her experiences, about her world, and about God. As she begins to understand herself and matures in her ability to choose between right and wrong, she also begins to understand the concept of repentance. Though she's been trained to say "I'm sorry" since she was a preschooler, true repentance comes through understanding a choice and realizing, with pangs of guilt, that she has made the wrong one. Repentance of sin demonstrates a child's awareness of her conscience and the voice of God helping her choose right instead of wrong.

These years of discipleship are critical. Third and fourth graders need both support and independence. They need to hear the experiences of others and be given opportunities to ask questions. Our prayer is that the words they have heard since infancy have taken root in their hearts so they might become convinced of the faith they have witnessed in others around them.

Champion God's Calling: Ages 11-12 Years (5th and 6th Graders)

He lies on his bed staring at the line of posters of his favorite athletes, dreaming about the day he'll be drafted into the professional league. She reviews the video she's just taken of herself strumming a guitar and singing an original tune before begging her parents to allow her to upload it to YouTube. He offers a sheepish smile as he places the slightly burned dinner he made by himself on the table for his family . . .

DEVELOPMENT OF 5TH AND 6TH GRADERS *(Ages 11–12 Years)*

Discipleship Direction: Champion God's Calling

Fifth and sixth graders express their identity through personal choices and peer relationships. Empower them in developing a personal relationship with God. Nurture their commitment to follow Christ. Foster their connections within a Christian community. Encourage them to recognize and utilize their God-given talents for His glory.

Cognitive and Behavioral Development	Emotional, Social, and Moral Development
• demonstrate individual preferences for learning environments ranging from loud, energetic groups to quiet, reflective spaces • desire to gain knowledge through discussion of topics of interest • like competition when they are successful and can demonstrate their skills • display abstract thinking by understanding concepts not tied to physical objects • apply deductive reasoning to anticipate outcomes • remain reliant on concrete experiences for understanding • need challenges and opportunities to demonstrate developing skills • recognize differences between their thoughts and beliefs and those of others	• desire independence but also acceptance by peers • identify heroes and those they desire to model • believe that right and wrong are based on rules, laws, and obedience • desire to assist in creating the boundaries and consequences; need a reason to follow rules • are influenced in attitude toward self by acquisition of skills and acceptance by others • develop attitudes toward social groups and institutions (school, church, organizations) • need firm, loving boundaries to provide a secure environment where they are supported and encouraged while simultaneously held accountable for actions

Preteens express their unique identities through individual choices and peer relationships. Guide and equip them toward a personal relationship with God and commitment to a Christian community.

Though they have not fully entered adolescence, preteens begin to practice for adulthood as they imagine their future identities. He isn't yet independent, but he desperately wants to be. She tries to live and make decisions in emulation of those a few years older, but she isn't quite mature enough for those situations. And as these emerging teenagers reach this milestone in their discipleship, they are making decisions that will affect the trajectory of their path. As preteens are in the process of identity formation, champion God's call on their lives to become more like Christ by loving God and loving others well.

In recent years, many school districts in the US have changed the way they approach this group of students. Fifth and sixth graders used to be "kings and queens of the hill" in elementary schools. Now some have been moved into middle school/junior high buildings or given their own separate spaces to allow for this unique period in their development. Approach this time in preteens' discipleship as singular as they leave childhood behind and move toward the formation of their own special identities.

As a child moves toward puberty and the onset of adolescence, her desire for relationships is in transition. As she moves toward placing more importance on seeking acceptance from her peers, a fifth or sixth grader can develop a personal relationship with God that is her own. It's during these years that the framework by which she sees herself, others, and the world—and how those things interact—becomes solidified. By the time she reaches age thirteen, a child can follow Christ because of her own convictions, not just because the adults in her life want or expect her to. She has a faith of her own.

While he can begin to piece together abstract ideas, he needs guidance from you and other caring adults to help him make sound decisions. Create a safe space where he can discuss his thoughts, ideas, doubts, and struggles. He will need help to correctly construct abstract concepts. The word *help* is used intentionally here. This is not a time for you to swoop in and do it for him. At the same time, do not overchastise him for something he has done wrong. Walk alongside him. Point out the potential pitfalls. Give him a helping hand when he's leaning too far one way or the other. Preteens need the opportunity to put their faith into action so they can build the self-confidence they need to place their identity fully in Christ.

Trusting God with the Journey

Though we have identified a goal and directions toward that goal, discipleship is not like a factory in which we place an infant on the assembly line of education and thirteen years later see her emerge as a perfectly formed follower of Christ. As you know, each child is uniquely created in God's image and is on his or her own journey toward Christ. Some children express greater interest in learning about God than others. Some children have experiences that cause them to doubt God's existence. Some children are more accepting, while others lean toward skepticism.

> *Discipleship is not like a factory in which we place an infant on the assembly line of education and thirteen years later see her emerge as a perfectly formed follower of Christ.*

How do we account for each child and their unique discipleship journey? By imitating the GPS—providing alternative routes in the event of a roadblock or detour. When the destination is known, a map allows for variety. Your work is to guide children toward Jesus. Trust that as you and your child journey along the discipleship map, you are partnering with the Holy Spirit. Your work does not guarantee a child's faithfulness—even Jesus had a disciple who failed to remain a follower—but your intentional guidance can bear much fruit.

One of the challenges of the discipleship map is for children to develop their own faith rather than relying on or adopting the faith of their parents or other influential individuals. Becoming more Christlike requires a child to have her own personal faith and active relationship with God. My hope is that the discipleship map can help a caregiver direct a child toward a lifetime of following Christ—one filled with joys and sorrows, peacefulness and struggles, but always striving toward and becoming more like Christ.

Although we identified a destination for the discipleship map, this is not the end. Discipleship is a lifelong journey. Along the way a child continues to mature in her beliefs, deepen in her understanding, and grow in her commitments. These seven legs of the journey can set a child on a trajectory for a life with God.

TYING IT ALL TOGETHER

As Jesus entered the final year of His earthly ministry, His instructions to the Twelve became more direct and challenging. His expectations of the disciples increased as He prepared to leave them to carry on His work.

> Then he [Jesus] said to them all: "Whoever wants to be my disciple must deny themselves and take up their cross daily and follow me. For whoever wants to save their life will lose it, but whoever loses their life for me will save it. What good is it for someone to gain the whole world, and yet lose or forfeit their very self? Whoever is ashamed of me and my words, the Son of Man will be ashamed of them when he comes in his glory and in the glory of the Father and of the holy angels."
> LUKE 9:23-26

As Jesus prepared to give up His life for the sins of the world, He prepared His disciples for a life of self-denial and self-sacrifice. A life of loving God and loving others. A life lived with an eternal perspective rather than an earthly one.

The goal of discipleship is not to raise mediocre, milquetoast believers who follow Jesus when it's convenient and socially acceptable. The goal of discipleship is for all of us to become more like Christ, willing to deny ourselves the things that trap us in this world. The goal of discipleship is that every aspect of our lives will be submitted to the lordship of Christ.

Jesus provides an example of raising the level of expectations for these twelve men. How does this translate to children, specifically in the first thirteen years of life?

PUTTING IT INTO PRACTICE
Questions for Reflection

1. Reflect on your own discipleship journey.

    • How does this discipleship map match your own experience? How was it different?

    • What areas of discipleship do you need to further develop in your own life?

2. Review the discipleship stage of the children in your life.

    • How does the description provided match what you're observing in their lives?

    • Which leg of their discipleship journey causes you the most concern? Why?

CHAPTER 3

Learning and Studying God's Word

It was a Thursday morning ladies' Bible study. A dozen women had gathered in a church classroom to study Scripture together. They had used various Bible study materials over the years—booklets and videos mostly. But for about two months I had been leading them through the book of Ephesians and teaching them how to use different tools for interpretation. We compared different translations. We looked up key words in concordances and dictionaries. One week we reviewed a Greek-to-English translation so they could see Scripture in its original language and how Bible translation works.

And as I was pointing out that a particular Greek word had appeared repeatedly in a section of text, one of the ladies—Helen, a woman in her midsixties—began to cry.

"Why has no one ever taught this to me before?" she finally burst out.

Helen had been raised by Christian parents in the same Christian community in which she was still active. She had attended hours of worship services, heard thousands of sermons, and participated in many activities. Her faith in God was real and her commitment to Christ was true, but in that moment she realized that for her entire life she had relied on someone else—devotional materials, a teacher, a preacher, a Bible study booklet—to tell her what the Bible meant. She knew stories, songs, and texts found in God's Word, but she had never been equipped to study God's Word.

In that moment, I was convicted by her question. First, I realized that few adults feel adequately prepared to delve into studying the Word of God so that they can interpret it accurately and apply its teachings appropriately. Then I realized that it wasn't enough to equip adults with tools for biblical interpretation and application. Instead, learning to read, study, and interpret the Bible *must* begin in childhood.[1] The Bible is God's Word. It is authoritative for our entire lives and across every circumstance. I would argue that reading it, studying it, and meditating on it is more valuable than learning multiplication tables or spelling words or state capitals. We have often failed to provide our youngest disciples with the foundational knowledge or essential Bible skills necessary to answer questions or navigate situations, however.

Why?

Because many adults do not feel equipped to teach the Bible to children or help children learn how to study and interpret Scripture.

The Bible contains sixty-six books, more than thirty-one thousand verses. It takes nearly seventy hours to read in one sitting.[2] It can be overwhelming to think about teaching the Word of God to others when you have failed to fully understand it yourself. But in the same way we help children prepare to learn how to solve algebraic equations by first teaching them how to count or teach them to read sophisticated literature by first introducing their letters, we can raise disciples to know the Word of God by starting with the basics. We begin by focusing on God.

The Story of God

God is the main character in the Bible and of every story we tell!

When we teach children the Bible, the focus can easily become repeating the same Bible stories and the details surrounding the human characters. We can feel confident that learning has occurred when a child can recall the names of people and places and details about numbers and nations. But too often we fail to focus on this question: *What does this story teach us about God?* Children may be able to describe the actions of Abraham, Esther, Peter, or Priscilla, yet rarely describe the activity of God found in these same stories.

The hero of every Bible story is God. Though Moses, Mary, Deborah, and Daniel represent characteristics that children should possess, these attributes originate with God. We want children to learn about faithfulness, courage, integrity, and love, but do we teach children that it is *through God's power* that these qualities can be demonstrated in their lives? When teaching the stories of the Bible, focus the child's attention on the actions of God and what can be learned about the character of God in the story.

One way to accomplish this is by beginning each story by telling children what they will learn about God in that story. (For example: The story of Joseph is God's story of faithfulness and protection. The story of Hannah is about God's compassion and care.) It is also accomplished by asking a child to share a characteristic of God she discovers in the stories or what she learned about God from the story. Though it is important to rear children to know the contents of the Word of God, it is even more important that they know about the God who provided that Word.[3]

God's Big Story

Helping children understand God's big story will also help them further understand the nature of God. Various patterns are used to describe the Bible's metanarrative—the overarching narrative of Scripture—but a simple one can help children begin to put the pieces of the story of God together:

Creation → Fall → Promise → Christ → Church → New Creation

All the stories and texts of Scripture fall into one of these six categories. Together they show God's perfect plan for the world. By age thirteen, the key stories that make up this narrative should be second nature. Children should know them better than stories in popular culture. They should also be able to recognize that these stories are part of their greater story in God's Kingdom—that they are part of God's ongoing story.

In early childhood, children don't comprehend the concept of time—past, present, future. Everything that is supposed to happen in the future—whether a month from now or a year from now—will happen "tomorrow" in their minds! Everything that happened "a long time ago" is thrown into one big pot of history. As we teach the Bible stories to these youngest learners, their imaginations will have Isaac, David, Lydia, and Zacchaeus all living in the same town just a few blocks from one another. As they develop an understanding of time and a perspective of history, they can begin to categorize events in order using the birth of Jesus as the center. By framing the events of the Bible within its overarching story, you're helping children realize that this story is given to us to help us understand God's plan from Creation to New Creation.

JESUS' METHOD: INTENTIONAL INSTRUCTION

For approximately three years, Simon Peter, James, John, and nine others were the primary recipients of Jesus' instruction, both individually and in a group. The preparation of the Twelve was not through some supernatural education formula. Instead, Jesus employed a method that mirrors how we can disciple children: through deliberate and gradual learning.

Jesus connected their learning to their direct experiences. He called Peter, a fisherman, to "fish for people" after a miraculous catch of fish (Luke 5:1-10). Jesus brought them to meals with "tax collectors and sinners" to help them understand God's love (Luke 5:29-31). He demonstrated His power and identified the disciples' need for a maturing faith in calming a storm (Luke 8:22-25).

Jesus used brief stories about everyday life—parables—to teach the disciples about the Kingdom of God. He told stories of a farmer planting crops (Luke 8:4-15), a Samaritan caring for his enemy (Luke 10:30-37), a woman celebrating the recovery of a coin (Luke 15:8-10), and a banquet with the outsiders of society becoming the honored guests (Luke 14:15-24). Each story progressively nudged the disciples toward insight into God's upside-down Kingdom.

Jesus also taught the Twelve how to act as citizens of God's Kingdom. In His "Sermon on the Plain" (Luke 6:20-49) Jesus taught them to trust God to meet their needs and help them love enemies, forgive others, and obey the commands of God. As they traveled with Jesus, the Twelve would be challenged to seek the Kingdom (Luke 12:31), leave everything, and carry their cross to follow Him (Luke 14:25-27). He was preparing them to give their lives to disciple others (Matthew 28:18-20).

Incremental, Age-Appropriate Learning

An infant begins receiving nourishment by drinking milk. Feeding them only milk for their first thirteen years of life would leave them malnourished and underdeveloped. But you also don't feed a two-month-old baby sirloin steak. Rather, incrementally, various foods are introduced. Fruits and veggies are mashed or pureed for them until the infant can chew. Slowly and deliberately their diet expands. Though it may seem like every lunch and/or dinner for your five-year-old consists of macaroni and cheese and chicken nuggets, those meals are still quite a bit different from the milk with which he started. By age eight, he can consume a wider range of foods, cutting his own food into bite-sized pieces. By the time he reaches adolescence he can consume a diet similar to that of an adult. What's more, he can learn how to cook simple meals. By age thirteen you have a relatively close approximation of an adult, as it pertains to nourishment. Your preteen still needs guidance in making wise choices, but he is ready to enjoy a rib eye.

The metaphor should be obvious. In the same way that children incrementally develop an ability to eat and enjoy food, they incrementally develop a means by which to consume the Word of God. At the end of Hebrews 5, the writer is frustrated at the lack of spiritual maturity he has encountered. The author writes,

In fact, though by this time you ought to be teachers, you need someone to teach you the elementary truths of God's word all over again. You need milk, not solid food! Anyone who lives on milk, still being an infant, is not acquainted with the teaching about righteousness. But solid food is

for the mature, who by constant use have trained
themselves to distinguish good from evil.

Therefore let us move beyond the elementary
teachings about Christ and be taken forward to
maturity.

HEBREWS 5:12–6:1

Elementary teachings lay the foundation for discipleship.
They're not sufficient for a lifetime of nourishment, but once
they have been learned, they can lead a child on the path
toward spiritual maturity.

The simple yet foundational truth of God is the milk. It
begins by introducing the name of God in infancy and continues by introducing stories that correspond to the age of the
child and their readiness for information. Because children are
concrete learners, we focus on teaching them the stories found
in the Bible. The best stories for this are those with details that
are connected to children's experiences or described in ways
that connect to their lives. As you teach these stories, connect
them to God's big story and remind children that their lives
are a continuation of this story, as we are the people of God.

Some of the stories we're familiar with from the Bible—
perhaps stories that were taught to us as children—take on
new meaning as we read them again when we're older. The
same is true for children. There are stories they need to hear
and read again and again. The beautiful thing about God's
Word is that greater understanding of His character and
work in the world is increasingly revealed to us over time.

For example, take the story of Creation. Introduce toddlers to the truth that God created the whole world. Preschoolers can learn that God created everything in six days with all the animals—the birds and the tigers and the puppy dogs—capturing their attention. Then when a child visits a zoo, talk about the diversity of God's creation as she explores animals with a sense of wonder and awe. In elementary school, as she studies science, the Creation story begins to take on an advanced meaning. She begins to understand how God's creation works together to sustain life. The sun nourishes plants. Rain brings nutrients to the soil. Animals eat plants or other animals. Life sustains life. It's still the same Creation story that she heard when she was in preschool, but now she's discovering a deeper meaning. By the time a child is introduced to scientific theories of the creation of all things, our intention is that she firmly believes that God is the Creator, and she can reconcile her faith with what she is learning in school.

Though there are stories to teach again and again, some Bible stories are best shared with children when they have an increased vocabulary and a better understanding of their world and experiences. For example, preschoolers can learn the story of God promising a son to Abram and Sarai and the birth of Isaac in their old age (Genesis 21). But Abraham preparing to sacrifice Isaac (Genesis 22) is a more complicated story that takes wisdom and maturity to comprehend. This story can cause fear in preschoolers and be misunderstood by elementary-aged children.

GOD'S BIG STORY FOR CHILDREN *(Old Testament)**

Age Range	Creation *(Genesis 1–2)*	
CORE TRUTH	**God created everything including you and me.**	
Establish God's Foundation: 0–12 Months (Infants)	• God loves me.	. . . .
Demonstrate God's Love: 1-2 Years (Toddlers)	• God created everything.	. . . .
Share God's Story: 3-4 Years (Preschoolers)	• God created everything in seven days.	. . . .
Engage God's Community: 5-6 Years (Kindergartners)	• God created everything and it was good. • God created all people and it was very good.	. . . .
Teach God's Truth: 7-8 Years (1st and 2nd Graders)	• God created Adam and Eve. • The Garden of Eden was perfect.	. . . .
Reinforce God's Commands: 9-10 Years (3rd and 4th Graders)	• In the beginning God created the world. • God is eternal. • God created us to be in relationship with Him.	. . . .
Champion God's Calling: 11-12 Years (5th and 6th Graders)	• God created a world that demonstrates His wonderful design and order. • God created all people in His image. • There was a perfect relationship between Adam, Eve, and God in the Garden.	. . . .

Note: As a child progresses from age to age, they build upon the knowledge and skills from earlier stages.

*The framework and list is representative rather than comprehensive. It helps put the stories of Scripture within the greater narrative of the Bible.

	Fall (Genesis 3–11) Sin ruined God's perfect creation.	Promise† (Genesis 12—Malachi) God made a promise to save the world.
-12 mos. ▶		
1-2 yrs. ▶	• God always loves me.	• God loves everyone.
3-4 yrs. ▶	• Adam and Eve disobeyed God. • God saved Noah and the animals. • Rainbows are a sign of God's promise.	• God keeps His promises, so follow God and obey His commands. • (Abraham, Isaac, Joseph, Moses, Joshua, Ruth, Hannah, David, Elijah, Esther, Daniel, Jonah)
5-6 yrs. ▶	• Adam and Eve sinned in the Garden of Eden. • God punished those who did not obey Him, but Noah obeyed God and was saved.	• God loves us and has a plan for His people. • Abram answers God's call. • (story of Moses: birth, calling, plagues, Red Sea, Ten Commandments, wilderness, Promised Land)
7-8 yrs. ▶	• Adam and Eve were tempted into sin. • God loves us even when we disobey. • People built the tower of Babel to glorify themselves, not God.	• The history of the people of God in the Old Testament: Abram → Isaac → Jacob → Joseph → Moses → Joshua → Judges → Saul → David → Solomon → Daniel → Esther
9-10 yrs. ▶	• Sin entered the world through Adam and Eve's disobedience. • Sin separates us from God's presence.	• *Covenant:* God establishes His people through Abram. • *Exodus/Tabernacle:* God leads His people. • *Judges:* People sin, repent, and are saved. • *Kings/Temple:* The people of God desire to be like other nations. • *Prophets/Exile:* Prophets call people to remember God's commands and repent. They also point toward Jesus.
1-12 yrs. ▶	• Cain killed his brother Abel. • God held Cain accountable for his attitude and his actions. • God gave grace to Noah while still judging the sin in the world.	• *Connecting the Old Testament to the New Testament:* both include covenant, law, sacrifice, sin, repentance, restoration, and prophecy.

†This section of the Old Testament can be further divided into: Covenant, Exodus/Tabernacle, Judges, Kings/Temple, and Prophets/Exile.

GOD'S BIG STORY FOR CHILDREN *(New Testament)* *

Age Range	Christ *(Gospels)*
CORE TRUTH	**God the Son, Jesus, came to earth to die on a cross to save the world by forgiving our sins.**
Establish God's Foundation: 0-12 Months (Infants)	• Jesus loves me.
Demonstrate God's Love: 1-2 Years (Toddlers)	• Jesus is God's Son. • Jesus did great things.
Share God's Story: 3-4 Years (Preschoolers)	• Jesus' birth • *miracles*: feeds five thousand, heals a paralyzed man, calms a storm • *parables*: lost sheep, Good Samaritan • Jesus' death, burial, and resurrection
Engage God's Community: 5-6 Years (Kindergartners)	• Jesus in the Temple at age twelve • *miracles*: blind man, deaf man, ten lepers • *parables*: wise/foolish builders • Triumphal Entry/Palm Sunday
Teach God's Truth: 7-8 Years (1st and 2nd Graders)	• birth of John the Baptist • Jesus resists temptation. • Jesus calls the disciples to follow Him. • *miracles*: catch of fish, walking on water, official's son, widow's son • *parables*: sower/soils • upper room/Last Supper • great commission and Ascension
Reinforce God's Commands: 9-10 Years (3rd and 4th Graders)	• *baptism*: Jesus is the Messiah, the Son of God, who takes away our sin. • *miracles*: Jairus's daughter, bleeding woman, Transfiguration • *parables*: lost sons (prodigals), talents, rich man and Lazarus • *teaching*: Sermon on the Mount • Judas's betrayal, arrest/Gethsemane, Peter's denial and restoration
Champion God's Calling: 11-12 Years (5th and 6th Graders)	• Jesus is fully God and fully man. • *baptism*: God the Father, Son, and Spirit • *miracles*: demon-possessed man, raising of Lazarus • *parables*: unmerciful servant, worker and wages, rich fool, wedding feast • *teaching*: cost of discipleship, woman at the well, Peter's confession • Jesus washes the disciples' feet. • Jesus cleanses the Temple. • road to Emmaus

Church *(Acts, Epistles)*	New Creation *(Revelation)*
God's people, who show others God's love and tell them about Jesus, are the church.	**One day, Jesus will return, and we will live with Him forever in heaven.**

	Church *(Acts, Epistles)*	New Creation *(Revelation)*
0–12 mos. ▶		
1–2 yrs. ▶	• God's people love me.	• God made everything.
3–4 yrs. ▶	• Church is any place where we worship God and learn about Jesus with others who love God. • The church is God's family, who love me too.	• Heaven is God's home.
5–6 yrs. ▶	• Peter and John heal a lame man. • Paul, Silas, and the Philippian jailer • *Epistles*: fruit of the Spirit	• Heaven is a perfect place.
7–8 yrs. ▶	• The Holy Spirit comes on Pentecost. • birth of the church • Saul's conversion • Peter in prison • Paul's missionary journeys • *Epistles*: body of Christ	• Heaven is where we will live with God forever. • Christ will return to take us to heaven.
9–10 yrs. ▶	• Peter's sermon on Pentecost • Philip and the Ethiopian • *Epistles*: lessons from James and Peter	• description of new heaven and new earth
11–12 yrs. ▶	• stoning of Stephen • Paul in Athens • Paul's arrest, shipwreck, imprisonment • *Epistles*: teaching from Paul's letters	• hell and judgment • tree of life in heaven

Note: As a child progresses from age to age, they build upon the knowledge and skills from earlier stages.
*Each year children should learn about Jesus' birth, Jesus' life and ministry, and Jesus' death, burial, and resurrection. The contents in the chart provide types of stories that connect with the discipleship focus of each age group.

Some of the parables and teachings of Jesus and most of the Psalms, Prophets, and Epistles require the ability to understand abstract concepts. Since most children don't develop this ability until late childhood or early adolescence (ages eleven to thirteen), we can delay introducing some material until they are older. My encouragement is that when you introduce children to a commonly used text like Psalm 23 or the fruit of the Spirit (Galatians 5:22-23), connect them to Bible stories that further illustrate the concepts (see an example in the next chapter). This helps connect the abstract concepts and vocabulary they do not yet fully comprehend to concrete examples they can understand.

We also need to acknowledge that some stories in the Bible just aren't appropriate for kids. In the same way we discern which TV shows, movies, and video games a child is allowed to view based on the rating and content, we should be discerning regarding the Bible stories we share with them at which ages. There are ways that these stories can be "sanitized"—removing elements that are inappropriate for children. Presenting a sanitized version of the story can change the meaning of the story and obscure the reason the story is included in Scripture. If you deem it necessary to introduce a story that contains violence or sexual situations, focus a child's attention on what the story teaches about the character of God.

When God gave the command to parents and the community to teach children, the core of that was to teach them to "love the LORD your God" (Deuteronomy 6:4-9). Rather than attempting to introduce every story of Scripture, we would do well to prepare children for meat by building a foundation of love for God and familiarizing them with stories from each section of God's big story. The "God's Big Story for Children" chart identifies key stories for each age group under the six big story categories. This is not an exhaustive list, but rather can help parents and children's ministry leaders focus their attention on key stories at an age-appropriate level.

From Listening to Bible Stories to Becoming Bible Students

One of the ways we underestimate children is in their increasing ability to learn on their own. In today's world it is not unusual for toddlers to have an electronic device—a smartphone or tablet—in their hands. By the time children are five, they are pros at looking stuff up online and finding information. If we give them the right tools and teach them some basic skills, they will have the ability to engage their own curiosity about God's Kingdom.

This journey starts with a child's love to have stories read to them. Begin with books that introduce the concept that God loves them. As he grows into a toddler and then preschooler, read simplified stories from the Bible. Remember, your priority is to give him a familiarity with the stories of the Bible and to help lay the foundation of recognizing God's character. You want to show how God is the hero of the story and emphasize His ongoing presence, protection, and promises.

It's appropriate that these stories are just good stories to your child—stories he loves and wants to hear again and again. You're helping him fall in love with the Bible and, by extension, fall in love with God and His Kingdom. For a preschool child it's less about teaching him to *read* the Bible and more about giving him a *love* for the stories of the Bible, which will lead to a desire to read them for himself as he gets older.

As children begin to learn to read, what better way to have them practice their skills than to read the stories of the Bible? Begin with Bible storybooks that have simplified the language and sentence structure and use age-appropriate vocabulary words. As their reading abilities develop, you can have your child practice reading these stories to you. The habits they develop at an earlier age when someone reads them the stories of the Bible—maybe for a bedtime story every night—can continue. They can now take the lead when it comes to reading those stories. There's a sense of discovery that they'll find in these stories as *they* read them as opposed to just listening to them. This helps develop the discipline to spend time in God's Word every day.

Introducing Various Bible Translations
Around age seven a child can transition from Bible story-books to reading a young reader's version of the Bible. One example is the New International Reader's Version (NIrV), which takes the translation work done for the New International Version and simplifies the sentence structure. Instead of compound sentences with lots of prepositional

phrases, the sentences are simplified to a third-grade reading level. This helps build confidence in a child that she, too, can read the Bible and understand it. At this time, she can learn Bible skills such as listing the books of the Bible in order and locating chapters and verses on her own. This is an important proactive step to take because it will help her take ownership in studying the Bible.

By the time children reach their preteen years, they can begin to understand the concept of Bible translation and recognize how different English translations tell the same story with different wording and sentence structure. Introduce them to the different approaches to Bible translation and explain why their great-grandparents might prefer one translation, while their ministry leaders use a different one. Have them read different translations of the same text to compare, and allow them to choose the translation they want to use for their own personal study. The "Bible Knowledge and Skills" chart provides an outline for parents and ministry leaders to follow in building confidence in Bible reading in childhood.

Building Biblical-Interpretation Skills

We don't live in the cultures that the stories of the Old or New Testament took place in. Some of the descriptions and illustrations used in the Bible do not make sense to kids living more than two thousand years after the events of Jesus' life on earth. So, as a child begins to read Scripture on their own, equip them with the resources to understand and interpret God's Word properly.

BIBLE KNOWLEDGE AND SKILLS

Age Range	Understanding of the Bible
Establish God's Foundation: 0–12 Months (Infants)	• I love the Bible.
Demonstrate God's Love: 1–2 Years (Toddlers)	• The Bible is God's book.
Share God's Story: 3–4 Years (Preschoolers)	• The Bible is God's special book for us.
Engage God's Community: 5–6 Years (Kindergartners)	• The Bible tells us God's story.
Teach God's Truth: 7–8 Years (1st and 2nd Graders)	• The Bible is God's Word. • God's Word is true.
Reinforce God's Commands: 9–10 Years (3rd and 4th Graders)	• The Bible is God's revelation to us.
Champion God's Calling: 11–12 Years (5th and 6th Graders)	• The Bible guides me in my developing relationship with God.

Note: As a child progresses from age to age, they build upon the knowledge and skills from earlier stages.

	Knowledge of the Bible	Training to Study the Bible
0–12 mos.	• *simple concepts*: God, Bible, love	• identify a Bible
1–2 yrs.	• *Bible concepts*: Jesus, creation	• identify a Bible • repeat three-word phrases/verses
3–4 yrs.	• simplified Bible stories	• ask to be read to / read specific Bible stories • recite verses with five to seven words
5–6 yrs.	• Bible stories and characters • *Two sections*: Old and New Testaments • simple application of Bible to life	• read from a Bible storybook with assistance • recite verses in simple sentences • identify key Bible stories and characters
7–8 yrs.	• Bible stories with more details • "God's big story" outline • identification of stories in the Old Testament or New Testament • Bible stories and characters related to their own life and experiences	• read Bible stories on their own (Bible storybook or NIrV, NCB) • recite core Bible verses • locate Bible verses with minimal help • list the books of the Bible in order
9–10 yrs.	• Bible stories in cultural context • new-to-them Bible stories and characters • Bible chronology • Scripture applied to life, including problems and struggles	• read the Bible daily with minimal prompting • recite Bible verses • locate Bible verses on their own • use Bible dictionary and map • ask questions about Bible stories
11–12 yrs.	• Bible stories with more details, including historical, cultural, and literary context • genres of Scripture • expand study of Scripture to include Psalms, Prophets, and Epistles	• read the Bible on their own (NIV, NLT) • recite sections of Bible passages • use Bible concordance • reference the Bible for answers to their questions

During their elementary years, introduce children to resources that help explain the content and vocabulary of the Bible. A Bible dictionary with pictures and images helps children understand the setting and context for the stories they're reading. Seeing an image of a first-century home helps the story of Jesus healing the paralyzed man make a lot more sense (*How did they get on the roof?*). A Bible atlas with maps and pictures of locations helps enhance and solidify what they are learning. These resources also help connect the stories in the Bible to what they're learning in social studies class. All these things bring to life the stories they're reading in new ways. Give young disciples access to Bible apps or Bible resource websites so they can investigate on their own.

As he shows a growing interest in learning more about the Bible, there are some steps of biblical interpretation a child can do with every Bible story. He can use the Five *W*s and an *H* (*who, what, when, where, why,* and *how*) pattern to identify the elements of the story. Once he has read the text and located the answers to these questions, he can list which elements of the story are confusing to him. He can identify the differences between the culture described in the Bible passage and the culture of today. Guide him in using resources to discover answers to his own questions, rather than giving him the answer.

As they mature into preteens, children can expand into reading a greater variety of biblical texts. Introduce them to the different genres of Scripture and how knowing the genre of a passage affects your interpretation of it. The poetry found in a psalm is to be interpreted differently than a command in a Gospel. The letters of the New Testament contain guidance for how we're to live as Christ followers but also provide commands that were specific for the culture of the time or for a specific congregation. Parables provide insight into the Kingdom of God, while prophecies remind the people of God about God's past commands and their future reality. Knowing these differences helps children understand how to read and interpret texts accordingly.

Preteens can learn how to research a biblical concept or theological word by reviewing its range of use in Scripture. They can compare parallel passages in the Gospels or connect a psalm to the historical event that inspired its creation. By locating events on a Bible timeline, they can see more clearly the unfolding of God's story throughout history and the patterns of God's faithfulness. They can learn to read Scripture amid a literary, historical, and cultural context so they can discover what the text meant at the time it was written.

Preteens will enjoy the process of mastering the knowledge they have been accumulating—practice makes perfect, as the saying goes. As they practice their interpretive muscles, they can move toward application to their own lives. As with everything during the preteen age, children need to be able to put into practice the things they've learned with the guidance of a caring adult. It's difficult to stand back and watch them stumble through things, but it's a big mistake to rush in and do it for them. Let them stumble and learn on their own. Remember, the goal is to help children develop their own faith, and if they can build confidence in putting the things they've learned into practice, it'll stick with them for the rest of their lives.

Encouraging Bible Memorization and Reflection

One of the best complements to learning God's Word throughout the course of childhood is verse memorization. Whether it's a short phrase for preschoolers or lengthy passages for preteens, hiding God's Word in their hearts establishes a firm foundation for faith (Psalm 119:11, 105; John 8:32).

During preschool, guide children in learning short sentences or sections of verses with vocabulary words that they understand. Five to seven words repeated on a regular basis grow roots in children's hearts that can last a lifetime. Add meaningful hand motions or sign language to help them connect the words with their concrete world. Sing the words in song form to make them easy to recall.

As children begin memorizing facts in school, encourage them to practice learning and reciting Bible verses. During these years, parents and churches can partner in identifying verses for children to memorize. Identify the Scriptures that articulate what you want them to believe about God, themselves, others, and the world.

It's important to encourage preteens to continue memorizing Scripture. Challenge them to memorize sections of Scripture instead of just individual verses. This helps them understand that the Word of God is not just a series of individual statements but rather a connected story of God's Kingdom.

A companion discipline to Scripture memorization is meditation—thoughtful reflection on God's Word. Age-appropriate daily devotion resources are one way to help children in early elementary school continue to read Bible stories and then consider how they connect to their lives. As they grow older, devotional resources can help them unpack abstract ideas and consider how Scripture applies in new situations and challenges they encounter.

Parents and churches can partner to connect what is taught at church with children's daily Bible reading. For younger children, repeating the same Bible story every day for a week helps them master the information and gives them the opportunity to ask questions and make connections. Older children can connect weekly lessons at church with other Scriptures about the same characters or themes. This type of partnership helps a child recognize the connection between the church and their daily life rather than thinking of the two as separate.

Raising Children to Know the Lord

When God began instructing His people how to worship Him, He provided the following guidance through Moses:

> These are the commands, decrees and laws the LORD your God directed me to teach you to observe in

the land that you are crossing the Jordan to possess,
so that you, your children and their children after
them may fear the LORD your God as long as you
live by keeping all his decrees and commands that I
give you, and so that you may enjoy long life. Hear,
Israel, and be careful to obey so that it may go well
with you and that you may increase greatly in a land
flowing with milk and honey, just as the LORD, the
God of your ancestors, promised you.

Hear, O Israel: The LORD our God, the LORD is
one. Love the LORD your God with all your heart
and with all your soul and with all your strength.
These commandments that I give you today are to
be on your hearts. Impress them on your children.
Talk about them when you sit at home and when
you walk along the road, when you lie down and
when you get up. Tie them as symbols on your
hands and bind them on your foreheads. Write
them on the doorframes of your houses and on
your gates.

DEUTERONOMY 6:1-9

In Jewish tradition religious education was not separate
from public education. All of life was religious education.
Parents were to *impress upon their children* God's command
to love and worship Him. As a child participated in everyday tasks—walking and talking, preparing meals, working
in a field—he learned about God. Through honoring the

Sabbath and being surrounded by the Word of God, he experienced God. And though parents were given the primary responsibility, *the entire community* was responsible for raising a child. At the center of that education was the intention to teach the child about God.

To be able to love, worship, and obey God, children must first learn about God.

How do parents raise disciples? By growing in the knowledge and study of God's Word. Who learns the most about a subject amid a lesson—the student or the teacher? After teaching in the church and in higher education for over twenty-five years, I can attest that it is the teacher. Every time I open God's Word to teach children, I learn something new.

Parents, if you have been struggling with ways to spend more time in God's Word, dedicate yourself to spending time reading and preparing to teach your children. Join a Bible study so you can continue to learn. Ask a ministry leader to equip you in how to study, interpret, and apply the Bible. Spend time with your kids studying God's Word and allowing their discoveries and questions to encourage you into deeper study. Both you and your children will benefit from this work.

May we not wait until someone is in their sixties—like Helen—to teach them how to study God's Word. Instead, train your child to learn the Scriptures from infancy so that she might develop knowledge of God through His Word that will lead to a relationship with God.

TYING IT ALL TOGETHER

Many of Jesus' teachings were in the form of parables—stories that Jesus told to illustrate what the Kingdom of God was like in concrete, earthly terms. One day as Jesus taught a crowd of people, including the Twelve, He told them a story about a farmer.

"A farmer went out to sow his seed. As he was scattering the seed, some fell along the path; it was trampled on, and the birds ate it up. Some fell on rocky ground, and when it came up, the plants withered because they had no moisture. Other seed fell among thorns, which grew up with it and choked the plants. Still other seed fell on good soil. It came up and yielded a crop, a hundred times more than was sown."

When he said this, he called out, "Whoever has ears to hear, let them hear."

LUKE 8:5-8

Jesus then took His disciples aside and explained to them the meaning of the parable.

"This is the meaning of the parable: The seed is the word of God. Those along the path are the ones who hear, and then the devil comes and takes away the word from their hearts, so that they may not believe and be saved. Those on the rocky ground are the ones who receive the word with joy when they hear it, but they have no root. They believe for a while, but in the time of testing they fall away. The seed that fell among thorns stands for those who hear, but as they go on their way they are choked by life's worries, riches and pleasures,

and they do not mature. But the seed on good soil stands for those with a noble and good heart, who hear the word, retain it, and by persevering produce a crop."
LUKE 8:11-15

If our hope is to plant the seed, the Word of God, deep into the good soil of a child, we must follow the example of Jesus, teaching her in ways she can understand and guiding her to discover the meaning of God's Word.

PUTTING IT INTO PRACTICE
Questions for Reflection

1. Review your family's weekly schedule.

   - When is your child receiving direct instruction in the knowledge of God?

   - How often are they reading or studying Scripture on their own or with you?

2. Review the resources (Bible storybooks, age-appropriate Bibles, devotional materials, etc.) available for your child to learn Bible stories.

   - Identify a list of resources you can use to teach your child how to understand Scripture (see appendix B).

   - What fears do you have about teaching your child how to learn and study God's Word? What steps could you take to overcome those fears?

   - What resources does your church community provide to partner with you in teaching your child? How could you use those resources on a regular basis in your home?

CHAPTER 4

Vocabulary of Faith

"Miss Teresa! Miss Teresa!"

Nathan was waving his arms from the back of the room, trying to get my attention just as forty or so elementary-aged children were settling into their chairs.

"Miss Teresa! Miss Teresa!"

I should have known by the twinkle in his eye that Nathan was up to something. By this time, I had been Nathan's children's minister for three years. He was bright, inquisitive . . . and ornery.

"Yes, Nathan. What is it?"

The kids quieted down long enough for Nathan to begin.

"Miss Teresa," he began, "if Adam and Eve were naked in the Garden of Eden . . ."

Yes, Nathan had just uttered the word *naked*. Giggles erupted.

". . . and heaven is supposed to be like the Garden of Eden . . ."

You can see where this is going, can't you?

". . . does that mean we will be naked in heaven?"

Giggling erupted into full-fledged laughter. The adult volunteers held in their own laughter. And Nathan beamed because he got to say the word *naked* twice at church.

With a little shake of my head and some laughter of my own, I responded, "Nathan, that is a great question!"

In that moment, I could have squelched Nathan's curiosity or chastised him for being disruptive. But instead, I recognized what was really happening—he was developing a vocabulary of faith!

What does it mean to "develop a vocabulary of faith"?

It begins by recognizing words that are used in Scripture. Though these words might be used in everyday conversation—such as *love, joy, peace*—their meanings take on an added depth within the context of God's Word. As children travel along the discipleship map, they learn how to define the words, use them appropriately, and identify their connection to Scripture. And as their vocabulary grows, a child not only comprehends the meaning of the words but also begins to use them to understand their relationship with God and others. Ultimately, a vocabulary of faith empowers a child to articulate their beliefs, share their understanding of

God with others, and mature in their comprehension of and relationship with God.

As children travel along the discipleship map, how do we help them develop a vocabulary of faith? What words should they be able to define and what concepts should they be able to comprehend at various ages? How do we help them transition from simple, concrete concepts to more abstract and profound insights?

Core Beliefs

As an activity in my college course Strategies for Teaching, I ask students to each write their name on a piece of paper and then give them ninety seconds to create an airplane out of it. Before they begin, I tell them that at the end of ninety seconds they will launch their airplanes, and the creator of the one that lands closest to the target will get a Starbucks gift card. (Gift cards for coffee are highly valued among college students!)

As they begin to fold (or wad) their papers into flying devices, I see them realize that I left out a key piece of information: what the target is. So they begin to ask: "Where is the target?" I simply smile and repeat the instructions: "When we reach the end of ninety seconds, you will launch your airplanes."

Slowly the realization strikes them that I am not going to tell them the target and they will just have to guess. Their eyes dart around the room, looking for an obvious target. As they launch their devices, the air is littered with paper. I look at my students and say: "This is what education in our churches looks like when we don't know the target."

They always get the point.

To help children recognize the target of their faith journey, we need to identify what *we* believe so they, too, can articulate their beliefs and live in accordance with them. What do we believe about God: Father, Son, and Holy Spirit? What do we believe about the Bible? What is the church, and what is the expectation for life as a follower of Christ? If we can't articulate those things for a child, how will we know that we are guiding them toward the goal?

Many church traditions have a creed they recite—such as the Nicene Creed—as their statement of belief. Other traditions have a series of statements provided by their denominations. Other churches, specifically those from nondenominational traditions, have commonality between churches but not universally accepted statements. Regardless of the church tradition of which you are a part, it is important for parents to partner with their community of faith to identify those statements and, if needed, create a version that uses kid-friendly vocabulary.

The example statement of faith for children provided on the next page might be helpful for you. It doesn't include everything we hope a child will believe, but it provides a series of declarations that are core Christian convictions and foundational for belief. Most importantly, a statement

EXAMPLE STATEMENT OF FAITH *(Core Beliefs) for Children*
WE BELIEVE . . .

God

There is one, holy God who loves us. We should love God with all our heart, soul, mind, and strength. God exists in three persons, the Trinity: Father, Son, and Holy Spirit.

God the Father created everything. God is perfect, loving, all-knowing, all-powerful, and all-present. God keeps all His promises. God never changes.

Jesus is God the Son. Jesus was born to a virgin and is fully God and fully human. Jesus came to teach about the Kingdom of God and show us how to follow God. Jesus never sinned. Jesus willingly died on a cross for our sins. Jesus was buried in a tomb and on the third day was raised from the dead. Jesus' resurrection shows the power of God over sin and death. Jesus ascended into heaven as our Savior, Lord, and King and awaits the day He will return.

God the Holy Spirit is alive and active in our lives. The Holy Spirit guides us to understand Scripture, feel guilt for sin, and become more like Jesus. The Holy Spirit gives us talents and abilities to glorify God and serve the church.

The Bible

The Bible is the true and inspired Word of God. The Bible teaches us about God and the story of God's perfect plan through Jesus. The Bible teaches us God's commands that He wants us to follow.

Humanity

God created all humans, male and female, in the image of God. God loves every person. All people have worth, value, and purpose. God created us to love and worship Him and to love one another.

Sin

God created a perfect world. Through Adam and Eve, the first man and woman, sin entered the world. The result of sin is separation from God, which leads to death. Everyone has sinned, and we cannot repair that sin without God.

Salvation

Our sins are forgiven because of Jesus' death on the cross. We are saved through God's gift of grace found in Christ alone. God wants everyone to hear the Word of God, believe in Him, repent of their sins, confess Jesus as Lord, and commit to a life of obedience demonstrated in the act of baptism.*

The Church

The church is God's Kingdom on earth. Everyone who believes in Jesus is part of the church that we also call the body of Christ. God desires us to use our God-given gifts to glorify Him and serve others. Jesus commands us to tell others the Good News and make disciples until He returns.

The Return of Christ

Jesus will return to establish a new heaven and a new earth. Those who do not believe in God will suffer judgment in hell. All who believe in God will have eternal life with God in heaven, where there is no sin or death.

*The statement about the inclusion of baptism may change based on the belief of your denomination or tradition.

of core beliefs gives you a target for guiding your child toward not only saying these words but also firmly believing them.

Vocabulary Development

I recently spent an evening helping my teenager study for her history test. She had a list of people, dates, and events related to FDR, the Great Depression, and the New Deal that she was trying to memorize. As I helped her study, I realized she didn't know some of the vocabulary used to define some of the terms. To understand the stock market crash, she needed to understand the term and concept of *stock*. She could have memorized the definitions to pass the text, but drawing a connection between the vocabulary and what she already knew helped her understand the information.

The development of a vocabulary of faith is parallel to the development of a child's full vocabulary. Being intentional about growing a child's vocabulary of faith begins with their experiences. A child learns the word *dog* by playing with their family pet. This four-legged, furry animal with two floppy ears, two eyes, a very wet nose, and a mouth that slobbers everywhere is a *dog*. When a child encounters another dog, she will point and say "dog." We affirm her vocabulary, acknowledging that she has used this word correctly in a new experience. She continues to develop her vocabulary when she sees other four-legged, furry animals with two ears, two eyes, a nose, and a mouth that are *not* dogs. She may point and say "dog," but someone responds with the correct label ("cat" or "horse" or "cow"). As she adds to her vocabulary, she will learn to distinguish between different types of information, placing new concepts into appropriate categories and simultaneously building an understanding of her world.

Throughout our lives, the neurons in our brains connect our experiences with words to create the building blocks of our vocabulary. Children rapidly absorb vocabulary words during their early years of life, retaining the words they hear most frequently. Toddlers begin to connect words with objects. Picture books and experiences build this vocabulary in preschool. As a child learns to read, his world expands with words, providing new opportunities for learning.

He learns the word and the definition, then he encounters it regularly in his reading and in conversations until he can utilize it properly on his own. Once a word is firmly established in his vocabulary, he can use it to begin to define and understand new words. With a vocabulary based on concrete experiences and understanding firmly in place, as children grow, they become able to understand abstract concepts in late childhood. Given the right environment, a child can learn ten new words a day from ages one through adolescence, resulting in a vocabulary of sixty thousand words.[1]

Because many words of faith are abstract concepts, a vocabulary of faith is built through the combination of stories and scaffolding.

FAITH VOCABULARY CHART

Age Range	God the Father	God the Son	God the Holy Spirit
Establish God's Foundation: *Demonstrate God's Love:* 0–2 Years (Infants, Toddlers)	• God	• Jesus	
Share God's Story: 3–4 Years (Preschoolers)	• Creator • Father	• God's Son	• Holy Spirit
Engage God's Community: 5–6 Years (Kindergartners)	• God Almighty	• Savior	• Spirit of God
Teach God's Truth: 7–8 Years (1st and 2nd Graders)	• Everlasting God • God Most High	• Christ • miracle worker	• Helper
Reinforce God's Commands: 9–10 Years (3rd and 4th Graders)	• Abba • Alpha and Omega	• God and man • King • Lord/Master	• Guide • Teacher
Champion God's Calling: 11–12 Years (5th and 6th Graders)	• I AM (YHWH)	• Emmanuel • human and divine • Messiah • Prince of Peace	• Advocate • Comforter • Counselor

Note: As a child progresses from age to age, they build upon the knowledge and skills from earlier stages.

	Characteristics of God	Faith Vocabulary	
0–2 yrs. ▶	• love	• Bible	
3–4 yrs. ▶	• great • powerful	• friend • helper • obey • prayer	
5–6 yrs. ▶	• good • kind • mighty • one and only God	• commandment • gentleness • goodness • kindness	• patience • trust • worship
7–8 yrs. ▶	• all-powerful • compassionate • faithful • glorious • perfect	• angels • baptism • believe • cross • crucifixion • devil • faithfulness • forgive	• heaven • joy • miracle • peace • resurrection • self-control • sin • truth
9–10 yrs. ▶	• all-knowing • everlasting • holy • merciful • righteous • unchanging	• confess • disciple • eternal life • faith • glorify • mercy	• praise • prophecy • repent • sacrifice • salvation • saved
11–12 yrs. ▶	• all-present • eternal • gracious • infinite • Judge • just • Shepherd • triune/Trinity • wise	• atonement • covenant • demons • gospel • grace • hell • imago Dei	• judgment • justification • pardon • revelation • soul • wrath

Bible stories help illustrate abstract concepts. For example, children can learn to memorize the fruit of the Spirit—love, joy, peace, patience, kindness, goodness, faithfulness, gentleness, and self-control (Galatians 5:22-23). But to understand the meaning of the fruit of the Spirit, they need a concrete illustration, such as a Bible story. For example, the parable of the lost sheep (Luke 15) teaches about joy; the story of Ruth (Ruth 1–4) teaches about kindness and faithfulness; the temptations of Jesus (Luke 4) illustrate self-control. Each story provides an opportunity to build a child's vocabulary.

Scaffolding involves introducing simple concepts over time that progressively build on each other. Take the word *grace*, an important term in our faith vocabulary, as an example. Grace is an abstract concept. How can we help prepare a preteen to comprehend God's grace for her? First, we teach her *yes* and *no* as a toddler. As a preschooler, she learns *good* and *bad*, which leads her to *right* and *wrong* in kindergarten. By early elementary school, she can comprehend the concepts of *sin*, *guilt*, and *forgiveness*, which provides the building blocks for understanding *repentance* and *consequences*. Simultaneously, her growing comprehension of God's love and holiness contributes to her matured understanding that lays the foundation for comprehending the profound concept of *grace*.

The "Faith Vocabulary" chart provided suggests key words and concepts for a child to learn at each stage along the discipleship map.[2]

JESUS' METHOD: EMBRACING QUESTIONS

One of Jesus' discipleship strategies was asking and answering questions. When the disciples woke Jesus in the middle of a terrible storm, He asked, "Where is your faith?" (Luke 8:25). Another time, when He asked, "Who touched me?" in a crowd of people, He created a teachable moment about faith (Luke 8:45). Yet another time He asked, "Who do the crowds say I am?" (Luke 9:18), which forced the disciples to articulate their own understanding of their rabbi. Like the disciples, kids benefit from being asked questions. It maximizes opportunities for new insight.

Jesus also welcomed questions. When the disciples asked Jesus to teach them how to pray, He gave them words to use (Luke 11:1-4). When they asked about the meaning of His teaching, He provided an explanation (Luke 8:9-15). And when they questioned others' motives, Jesus redirected their attention (Luke 9:49-50). Unlike Jesus, adults may not feel equipped to answer every question a child asks, but rather than ignoring them or placating them with a few words, allow kids' questions to create a space for discussion and engagement. Use these opportunities to help children discover the answers with you or investigate their question through research.

Asking and answering questions puts knowledge into practice, helping build a firm foundation for a lifetime of following Christ (Luke 6:46-49). When utilized alongside Jesus' other methods of discipleship, the practice of embracing thought-provoking questions can lead to increased understanding of God, His Word, and His ways.

Embracing Questions

Like Jesus' method of asking and answering questions with the Twelve, embracing questions is a way to help a child practice using their vocabulary of faith while also assessing how well they're learning the information. Sometimes it's as easy as asking a child for a definition of a particular word. Other times it's asking open-ended questions that give a child an opportunity to practice using her faith vocabulary.

In one of the children's ministry courses I teach, students are required to interview two children—one aged between five and seven and the other between ages ten and twelve. Students document the responses children give to fifteen open-ended questions. They ask questions such as these: "Why did God create people?" "What feelings do you have when you think about God?" "Think about a time you did something wrong—why did you do it?"[3]

During class discussion, students highlight the variety of answers, making note of the differences in vocabulary and understanding of these two age groups. Every time students share their reports, they express how much the kids they interviewed enjoyed answering their questions. Part of this might be that children enjoy the one-on-one attention of a college student. But also, children love for others to listen to them, especially when they're given time to share what they're learning. In these moments we're able to add to their understanding, correct any misunderstanding, and build their confidence in sharing the gospel.

One Sunday morning I was teaching a group of elementary-aged kids about the temptations of Jesus described in Luke 4. As we began, I asked if anyone could define the word *sin* for us. Eight-year-old Darius raised his hand high and said, "Sin is when you do something good." That answer was unexpected! I realized that for this young man, who had just started attending church a few months before, somewhere along the way he had heard the word *sin* and recalled the opposite. Fortunately, in that moment, I had the opportunity to gently correct his misunderstanding and affirm his desire to participate.

It was also an opportunity to remember that I should never take for granted that every child knows the definitions of the words that create our vocabulary of faith.

After you read kids a Bible story, ask questions—not just about the details of the story but also about the ideas and concepts. Ask them open-ended questions amid conversations. Encourage them to practice using their growing vocabulary and guide them when they stumble to say things well.

The "Questions and Prompts for Building a Faith Vocabulary" chart provides questions for conversations that can help build a child's vocabulary as she travels along the discipleship map.

QUESTIONS AND PROMPTS FOR BUILDING A FAITH VOCABULARY

Topics	Ages 3–6 Years
God	• What are some names for God? • What are some words that describe God? • What are some things God created?
Jesus	• What words describe Jesus? • What stories do you remember about Jesus? • Why did Jesus die on a cross?
Holy Spirit	• Who is the Holy Spirit?
Bible	• What are your favorite stories from the Bible?
Humanity	• Why did God create the world? • How can you show God you love Him?
Sin	• Think of a time you did something wrong. Why was it wrong? Why did you choose to do the wrong thing?
Salvation	• What do you do when you have done something wrong? • Why does God forgive you?
Church	• Why do we go to church?
Return of Christ	• How does someone go to heaven?
Relationship with God and Others	• Name the five people you love the most. • Name the five things that are the most important to you. • What do you say to God when you pray? • What feelings do you have when you think about God?

Note: As a child progresses from age to age, they build upon the knowledge and skills from earlier stages. These are examples of open-ended questions and prompts that provide an opportunity for children to use their own words to express what they are learning and coming to believe.

Topics	Ages 7–12 Years
God	• What are some names for God? • What do those names mean? • What are some words that describe God? • Describe the relationship between God the Father, God the Son, and God the Holy Spirit.
Jesus	• What words describe Jesus? • What do you believe about Jesus' life, death, burial, and resurrection?
Holy Spirit	• How does the Holy Spirit help you?
Bible	• What is the purpose of the Bible in your life?
Humanity	• Why did God create people? • What is God's purpose for your life?
Sin	• Think of a time you did something wrong. Why was it wrong? Why did you choose to do the wrong thing? • How do you resist temptation?
Salvation	• Describe how you feel after you have sinned. • How do you know God has forgiven you?
Church	• How are you using your gifts and talents to glorify God and tell others about Him?
Return of Christ	• Will everyone go to heaven? Why or why not? • If Jesus were to return today, would you be ready to go to heaven? Why or why not?
Relationship with God and Others	• Do you ever wonder if God exists? • What questions do you have about God and God's Word? • If you have an important decision to make, how do you make it? • What feelings do you have about God? • What types of things do you talk about with God? • How do you know that God loves you?

JESUS' METHOD: TEACHABLE MOMENTS

At times Jesus launched into a message to His followers without an external cue, but more often an event prompted Him to connect the knowledge of God to the reality of the circumstances. Jesus interwove teachable moments so seamlessly into the daily routines of the disciples' lives that it seems spontaneous. When we review the Gospels with this in mind, we see how intentional His teaching was. Jesus took advantage of moments when the Twelve were eating together and working together. He took advantage of times they were challenged by critics and adversaries. He took advantage of situations to reveal who God had created them to be, empowering them to live out their purpose.

One of these most well-known teachable moments came at a time born of a natural human reaction—hunger (Luke 9:10-17). Jesus had been teaching for a while and tried to withdraw to a remote place with His disciples, but the crowds kept following them. People kept coming and coming until the crowd had swelled to include thousands. So Jesus gave them what they both needed and wanted—His teaching. The disciples identified that a problem might soon arise, as there was no food nearby. As the day continued, people got hungry. A disciple pulled Jesus aside and pointed out to Him that He should send the crowd away so that they might find things to eat in the towns nearby. Jesus' response was for the disciples to feed the crowd. This, of course, is the shocking moment that made this teachable moment so successful. And don't miss this very important part of every teachable moment: A shocking, unexpected new perspective is presented to nudge people toward insight.

The disciples' response was to scramble to obey and then panic when they could only locate five loaves of bread and two fish—hardly enough to feed a crowd of thousands. But Jesus multiplied the food, providing enough for everyone to be full, with twelve baskets of leftovers besides. The disciples saw themselves facing an impossible feat. Their solution was to send people away and make them fend for themselves. But Jesus provided a new perspective and helped them understand that taking care of others—in this case, feeding them—is the nature of the Kingdom of God. And while we can't multiply loaves and fish with our hands (though that could be handy from time to time!), we can use difficulties and problems to help the children in our care see their tough situations through God's eyes. This almost always results in a new perspective.

Teachable Moments

Jesus used teachable moments to instruct the disciples. In the same way, parents and children's ministry leaders can use everyday moments to point kids to God and help them practice their vocabulary of faith.

Imagine you're on your way to school and your son is nervous about his upcoming spelling test. You could embrace that teachable moment and ask: "Do you think Jesus ever had to take a test? If He did, was He nervous?" Then see what kind of answers your child gives and allow that conversation to unfold. There's no right or wrong answer, but it provides an opportunity to help your child have a Christ-centered point of view about the event he's apprehensive about. It also helps him imagine Jesus in real-life situations like his own. That makes Jesus seem even more real, which is so important for a child.

Or let's say you have to tell your child that someone she loves has died. Embrace this opportunity for her to share how she feels. Remind her that when Jesus saw His friend Mary and others weeping because His friend Lazarus had died, He cried (John 11:35). Point her to the truth that Jesus joins her in her sadness but also to the hope that when Jesus returns, there will be no more death or sadness.

To embrace teachable moments, create environments that revolve around open, honest conversations. Practice listening well and being fully present. Slow down and pay attention to the prompting of the Holy Spirit. If this becomes your normal practice, then it's relatively seamless to move into and out of teachable moments. Big, soul-changing moments aren't the only teachable opportunities. Many little moments in every day can be used to point a child to Christ.

Seizing Teachable Moments

Grab their attention
with something unexpected.

Use a situation to start a conversation.

Address emotions
(concern, curiosity, anxiety, wonder, etc.)
by referencing the character of God.

Identify misplaced priorities.

Point to God's work in their life.

Responding to Challenges

A caution for parents and children's ministry leaders: When discussing difficult topics like death, violence, or abuse, we can sometimes do harm by trying to provide simple answers or give kids platitudes. In these hard teachable moments, listen more than talk. Allow the child to express what they are feeling and ask questions. Pray for the guidance of the Holy Spirit and for wisdom. Guide them to remember what they've learned about God's love and justice. Remind them that Jesus gave an example of what life is like in God's Kingdom and that He will return someday to set everything right.

At some point a child is going to ask you a question you don't know how to answer. Don't be afraid of these moments—embrace them! It's those moments that allow both of you to gain knowledge. First, you get to admit that you don't know everything and explain how you seek answers to your questions. This helps build her confidence that when she doesn't know the answer to something, she can ask for help and find the answer. Your response could be to search the Bible together or seek out wisdom from someone else. I hold an undergraduate Bible college degree, two master's degrees, and a doctor of ministry. Children still ask me questions I don't know the answer to. So when I respond, "That's a great question, and I don't know the answer," it's a joy to see the wonder on their faces when they realize we're going to discover something new together.

Fortunately, on the Sunday of Nathan's inquiry, I did have an answer. According to Revelation 7:9, we will be dressed, in robes! (Thanks, Holy Spirit, for bringing that to my memory at just the right time.)

TYING IT ALL TOGETHER

As Jesus was making His way toward Jerusalem, He was informed that His friend Lazarus was sick and close to death. Rather than hurrying to Bethany to heal His friend, Jesus remained where He was for two more days before continuing His journey.

On his arrival, Jesus found that Lazarus had already been in the tomb for four days. Now Bethany was less than two miles from Jerusalem, and many Jews had come to Martha and Mary to comfort them in the loss of their brother. When Martha heard that Jesus was coming, she went out to meet him, but Mary stayed at home.

"Lord," Martha said to Jesus, "if you had been here, my brother would not have died. But I know that even now God will give you whatever you ask."

Jesus said to her, "Your brother will rise again."

Martha answered, "I know he will rise again in the resurrection at the last day."

Jesus said to her, "I am the resurrection and the life. The one who believes in me will live, even though they die; and whoever lives by believing in me will never die. Do you believe this?"

"Yes, Lord," she replied, "I believe that you are the Messiah, the Son of God, who is to come into the world."

JOHN 11:17-27

Martha says she believes in the power of Jesus, in the resurrection, and that Jesus is the Son of God. But a few verses later, Martha shows her words do not yet match her understanding.

"Take away the stone," he [Jesus] said.

"But, Lord," said Martha, the sister of the dead man, "by this time there is a bad odor, for he has been there four days."

Then Jesus said, "Did I not tell you that if you believe, you will see the glory of God?"

So they took away the stone. Then Jesus looked up and said, "Father, I thank you that you have heard me. I knew that you always hear me, but I said this for the benefit of the people standing here, that they may believe that you sent me."

When he had said this, Jesus called in a loud voice, "Lazarus, come out!" The dead man came out, his hands and feet wrapped with strips of linen, and a cloth around his face.

JOHN 11:39-44

We are all like Martha. What we say we believe and how we act on those beliefs may not always be consistent. The life of discipleship is one of continuing to grow in our understanding of the vocabulary of our faith and acting in accordance with what we say we believe.

PUTTING IT INTO PRACTICE
Questions for Reflection

1. What declarations do your church or denomination use as their core belief statement? Is there a version of this statement that uses language that a child can understand?

2. What faith vocabulary words do you use on a regular basis?

3. Which words should you introduce to your child?

4. What questions have your children asked or might they ask that you are afraid to answer?

5. Ask your child, "What do you believe about God?" and see where that conversation leads.

CHAPTER 5

Spiritual Practices

I had been married for two weeks when my husband made an unsettling announcement at breakfast one Saturday morning.

"I have a nickname for you," he said, with an ornery look in his eye.

"Oh yeah?" I asked skeptically. "What's that?"

My husband then proceeded to violently beat the air with pretend drumsticks and head bang as he sang out, "Animal! Animal!" He was mimicking the famous rock-drumming character Animal from *The Muppet Show*.

I was confused and a little hurt. My stepdaughter began to giggle.

"What do you mean?" I asked.

He chuckled, "I love you, and you make so much noise in the morning when you are getting ready. You sound like Animal from the Muppets."

He then pantomimed opening and closing drawers and picking up and dropping things on the counter. It was an (unwelcome) revelation. I was merely going about my morning routine, as I had for many years. We were in our forties when we got married. I had lived alone for twenty-five years, so I had no idea that I was making so much noise. The things I was doing were just muscle memory at that point.

Pause for a moment and think about your own morning routine. What is the typical order in which you shower, brush your teeth, eat breakfast, exercise, and/or take care of a dozen other tasks you do at the start of each day? Most of them are probably completed without much thought. You rely on muscle memory. You put on your pants one leg at a time without considering which leg goes first. (Seriously, think about trying to put your pants on with the opposite leg first—you'd feel like you were falling over.) You tie your shoes in the same way. You likely have a certain approach you use when brushing your teeth. I evidently did all those things . . . while also making a lot of noise.

The patterns you use every day to dress, read, write, cut your food, and any of a thousand other things were formed during your childhood. Without this muscle memory, every moment of every day would require a lot of thought and energy. Instead, certain activities become as easy as it is to breathe. Every so often you're conscious of your breath, but not every instant.

How do we become aware of God in every moment of our day, allowing Him, rather than our natural inclinations, to guide our steps? How do we, as Paul encourages the believers in Rome, "offer [our] bodies as a living sacrifice" and "be transformed by the renewing of [our] mind[s]" (Romans 12:1-2)?

Or, as Paul encourages the church at Colossae, "set [our] minds on things above, not on earthly things" (Colossians 3:2)?

How do we follow the two greatest commandments—love God and love others—in such a way that it becomes as natural to us as breathing, walking, or brushing our teeth?

Spiritual habits—also called Christian disciplines or spiritual practices—are activities to create space for God to do His work to form us into the image of Christ. Christians undertake spiritual practices over the course of their lives, not only because it's an act of obedience to God but also because it cultivates a deeper relationship with Him.

We can carry the habits we build in childhood with us our whole lives. That makes it extremely important to develop spiritual practices and holy habits from a young age.[1] What an awesome opportunity you have to create an eternity-lasting practice in your children! It's building muscle memory that eventually becomes second nature. And though following Christ is never promised to be easy, spiritual disciplines can make the Christian lifestyle more effortless, leaving us more room to focus on the tasks and challenges that God offers us as participants in His Kingdom.

This chapter will focus on nine spiritual practices that children can participate in along the discipleship map. The first four—prayer, adoration and praise, Christian community, and giving—are the most understood and practiced. The five practices that follow—silence and solitude, Sabbath keeping, journaling, fasting, and gratitude—provide further ideas for how children can be encouraged to create a space to develop their relationship with God. Two additional spiritual practices—studying God's Word and using talents and abilities to serve—are addressed in chapters 3 and 6, respectively.

The overarching practice for each is worship. Everything we do should ultimately be about elevating God above ourselves, the very definition of *worship* (John 3:30). These practices often overlap. In fact, I encourage you to help your kids identify ways these spiritual practices influence one another and build a muscle memory of practices that constitute a life of faithfully following Jesus.

1. Prayer

From the time a child is born, parents and others pray over the little one, voicing words to introduce them to the God who created and loves them. Let infants and toddlers hear you say the name of God, their name, and what you sound like when you have a conversation with God. Let them hear and see your reverence for God.

Once a child begins to speak on his own, encourage him to join you in saying short prayers: "God, I love you" or "God, thank you." As his vocabulary increases, the length and content of his prayers should mature. As he enters his preschool years, teach him to pray an "echo prayer" by repeating prayers after you, one phrase at a time. You can also teach him simple prayers to repeat at mealtimes, bedtime, and other moments of the day. Also give your preschooler an opportunity to word his own prayers, practicing the vocabulary of his faith. He may pray for every person he knows, stuffed animals, or cartoon characters, but through his prayers you can hear what he is concerned about and how he is understanding his relationship with God.

As a child grows older, guide her from self-centered or meal-centered prayers to a prayer life that extends beyond her daily requests. *Thank you* prayers are a good reminder that God has worked in her life that day but can tend to be a list of things that are all about her. *Help me* prayers acknowledge God's power in her life, but those also focus on her. Utilizing a prayer pattern may help children expand their prayer practice beyond prayers that focus on themselves.

One such pattern is ACTS (**A**doration → **C**onfession → **T**hanksgiving → **S**upplication). To pray using this pattern, begin with words that describe God and how you experienced God's character that day (*holy*, *awesome*, *powerful*). After you acknowledge God's greatness, confess your sins and how you fell short of obeying God that day. Through thanksgiving, recognize God's forgiveness and daily blessings. Conclude by bringing any requests before Him, praying for others before praying for your own needs.

Children can also be taught to pray spontaneously throughout the day in keeping with Paul's admonition in

1 Thessalonians 5:16-18, "Rejoice always, pray continually, give thanks in all circumstances; for this is God's will for you in Christ Jesus." As you drive down the road, thank God for the setting sun, changing leaves, or budding flowers. The moment you hear someone is sick, pray for God's healing and comfort. If your child is anxious about a test, lead him to pray for God's help in recalling the information. (*Note:* Make sure he's asking for recall of the information, not for God to supernaturally teach him the spelling words he didn't study!)

Help children build the spiritual practice of prayer so they can mature into having an ongoing conversation with God.

2. Adoration and Praise

This phrase, *adoration and praise*, describes activities that lift up God's name and give worth to God above all others.

Music is a common way to help children express their love for God while also learning His names and attributes. Singing about and to God isn't just for Sunday mornings or musical families but for all believers and during car rides, morning and nighttime rituals, or while doing chores. Many children love to sing, and some of the best times you can have with them will be singing songs at the top of your lungs. Make the most of their natural interest by choosing songs that connect with their age-level vocabulary, understanding of God, and preferred musical style.[2] Soon the words they sing to God in a song will become their everyday vocabulary about God's presence in their lives.

JESUS' METHOD: RELATIONAL CONNECTION

Jesus and the disciples experienced the original Christian community. They traveled, ate meals, and experienced struggles together. The Twelve saw Jesus model what He taught. They witnessed Him love His enemies. They watched Him withdraw to solitary places to spend time with God the Father. They were present when He healed lepers, consoled parents, and cared for outsiders.

Because of this relationship, the disciples heard words of comfort, words of challenge, and words of rebuke from Jesus. They didn't follow Jesus because it was easy and comfortable. Instead, they rose to His challenge to lay down their lives to follow Him. They repented when He confronted their sins. They attempted to protect Him from arrest, they mourned His death, and they celebrated His return. As Jesus called the Twelve to increasing levels of accountability, He reminded them of His love for them and continued to point them to the Father.

The relational connections Jesus developed with the Twelve were not just between Jesus and each disciple individually. He also encouraged them to love and support one another. He called them to account when they argued about their positions within the group (Luke 9:46-48) and within the Kingdom (Luke 22:24-30). He set an example for how to treat one another and others they would encounter (John 13:14). He prayed for their unity (John 17:20-23), knowing they would need to support one another and hold each other accountable for the message to spread.

Adoration and praise also come through statements about God. Help kids notice creation and the beauty of God's design. Point out things that are wondrous to behold, such as the sunrise with the pinks and purples and blues that God paints across the sky, or the sparkling silver and crystal trees on a wintry morning after a snow. Pause for a moment and enjoy the horizon filled with gold and orange leaves during an autumn afternoon, or the starry sky on a clear summer night. The beauty of God's design is all around us, and when you're proactive about pointing these things out to children, they can't help but express an awe and wonder about the greatness of God.

These actions of adoration move a child from knowing *about* God to knowing God. It moves them from being able to describe God and His characteristics to believing that He loves them and wants to be in a relationship with them. They were created for relationship with Him, so encourage that conversation between children and the One they should adore more than any other.

3. Christian Community

Every child has an ever-growing and ever-changing group of relationships. Throughout childhood, the primary relationship for a child is with his parents and other primary caregivers, followed by those who live in his household (siblings, extended family). As he begins to develop friendships with other adults, it is important that these relationships help point him to Jesus. As he begins to develop peer relationships, becoming friends with others who are also following Christ will affect his growth. We can learn about God and how to be the people of God through the experiences of Christian community (Acts 2:42).

Often the word *church* is used to describe a physical location, such as a building with a sanctuary and classrooms. But the word most often used in the New Testament to identify the body of Christ (*ekklēsia*) is best understood as an

assembly or gathering of people, not a location.[3] This definition of the church as the community of believers describes
anyone gathering, wherever they are, under Jesus' name to
do the work of God's Kingdom.

Parents needs to prioritize participating in the life and
activities of a Christian community. Jesus exemplified the need
for community—not just through the training of His disciples
but also by going to synagogue on the Sabbath and by encouraging others to meet. Jesus prayed in the upper room that
the Twelve would become one and that all believers would be
brought to complete unity in and through Christ (John 17:11,
22-23). Acts 2:42 describes the believers as having "devoted
themselves to the apostles' teaching and to fellowship, to the
breaking of bread and to prayer." To become like Christ, we
need the body of Christ. Build within your child the spiritual
practice of being involved with a church family.

When you consider your own childhood education,
which do you remember more: what you learned, or your
connection to the person you learned it from? Research demonstrates that a child can memorize pieces of information,
but there is a relational component to truly learning something.[4] We need to care about what we're learning and have
a positive relationship with those we're learning from.

Research also shows that children who have three non-
parent adult relationships in their lives—caring adults who
regularly invest in their lives—grow into more well-rounded
and healthy individuals.[5] A church community provides a
space in which children can connect with caring adults on a

regular basis. These adults become mentors, confidants, and assistants in raising disciples. In fact, before I became a step-mom to Lorelai, I was her mentor for several years after I met her (and her dad) through children's ministry. Once I became her stepmom, Chris and I encouraged her connection with other mentors in our Christian community.

Parents, invite your children's ministry leaders and volunteers to be involved in your child's life. Encourage them to find a mentor they can share their feelings with and ask questions. Champion those people in their lives and make it a weekly practice to meet with those people. Connect your child with other adults in the church through inviting a variety of adults (from college-aged students to young couples to widows) to share a meal with you. Encourage their friendships with peers at church. As a child moves from parents to peers as the primary influences in their life, it is helpful for them to have a group of Christian peers for mutual support through the teenage years and into adulthood.

4. Giving

Children are inherently generous—often more so than adults. Champion and encourage their desire to give to others. By encouraging this practice in their lives, you're teaching them that everything belongs to the Lord (Psalm 24:1). We are only temporary stewards of what God has provided.

In giving, remember your child watches and mimics your actions. He will notice when you put money in an offering basket or provide a meal to a family in need. From the time your child earns an allowance, train him to set aside a portion to give to God and discuss with him how this becomes a pattern for his life. As a family, identify items that you can give away when a need arises. Decide to receive fewer Christmas gifts so you can sponsor a child's meals or tuition in conjunction with an international mission organization. When he is selective about what he is willing to share or part with, use this as a teachable moment about how generosity sometimes requires sacrifice.

Partner with your church to provide opportunities to donate toys, canned goods, or other items to teach her about generosity. When they collect an offering for missionaries or a local ministry, encourage your child to do some chores for others as a way of fundraising for the offering. Encourage her friends who set up a lemonade stand by showing up and donating. Take every opportunity to teach children the spiritual practice of giving.

If we can be proactive about teaching kids the spiritual practice of giving, they can take this joy-filled exercise with them the rest of their lives.

5. Silence and Solitude

Children are surrounded by noise (audible and otherwise). Music, YouTube, conversations, video games, sporting events, text messages, extracurricular activities . . . your child is constantly bombarded with the noise of their environment and schedules. Encouraging them to develop the spiritual practice of silence and solitude can be helpful in building a relationship with God. This practice follows the example of Christ, who regularly withdrew from activity to meet with the Father (Luke 5:16).

Psalm 46:10 says, "Be still, and know that I am God." The Hebrew word that's translated as "be still" here (*rapa*) can more literally be translated "drop the hands" or understood as "to let go [of your grip]."⁶ The practice of silence and solitude is to separate ourselves from distraction so that we can focus our minds and hearts solely on God.⁷ Starting with as little as thirty seconds, we let go of our grip on our activities and allow God to fill our minds. Giving a child an opportunity to be still and sit in quietness helps her learn to be comfortable with simply sitting with God. For a child who is introverted, this time will be welcomed as an opportunity to connect with God. For a child who is extroverted, this may require more discipline, but it can be helpful for her to practice quieting herself so she can listen to God.

From the time a child is age three or four, identify a space within his room or somewhere in the home that is his "holy" space. A beanbag chair in the corner or a particular spot on his bed can be his place to sit and be still before reading a Bible story or praying. (*Note:* Please don't also make this his time-out location.) You can ask him to imagine God in heaven on a throne or look outside at God's creation. It may be difficult at first for him to learn to settle down (it's hard for us adults as well), but creating space for this practice early in life helps your child build a holy habit.

As they reach school age, children can stretch this time

from a minute to a few minutes or longer. You can teach them to take deep breaths in and out to help their bodies relax and focus on God. They can be guided by choosing a word that helps them focus on God—*awesome, majestic*—and repeat that in their minds. This practice helps them realize that God is always present.

When a child begins to show an awareness of her inner voice—her conscience—guide her in learning to quiet that voice and focus on God. A physical practice that can help her is called Palms Up, Palms Down.[8] Have a child open her palms upward and then ball up her fists, pretending that she's holding on to all the things that are bothering her. Have her turn over her hands and open them, imagining that all the things that are bothering her are dropping to the ground as she releases her concerns to the Lord. Have her turn her palms upward as a reminder that she is to listen to the Lord. If she gets distracted, have her ball up her fists again with what she begins to think about and turn her palms down when she's ready to release it. This practice helps the child release her worries and anxieties.

Silence and solitude can also be practiced with others in the family. Give a child a chance to find his or her own space in a room and guide your family through imagining God on His throne, focusing on a characteristic of God, or through the Palms Up, Palms Down exercise. This isn't a practice that comes naturally at first, or one which will be done perfectly. But over time it will help children develop a habit of focusing their minds and hearts on God and listening for God's "gentle and quiet whisper" (1 Kings 19:12, MSG).

6. Sabbath Keeping

In keeping the fourth commandment, "Remember the Sabbath day by keeping it holy" (Exodus 20:8), the Jewish community ceased work from sundown on Friday to sundown on Saturday. It was a reminder of God's rest after the days of Creation. It was to build the habit of relying on God, not themselves.

In our current culture, busyness can become an idol—what we choose to worship over God. Sabbath keeping is a reminder that God should be the center of our schedules. Whether you honor the Sabbath on Saturday or Sunday, take twenty-four hours to rest from your daily schedule and rhythm and use that time to worship God. Rest from work and other chores so that you have time to enjoy loving others through good food and recreation.

One family I know begins their Sabbath on Friday evenings with a feast. They eat a meal together, often inviting others to join them. They take their time as they eat, enjoy conversation, and always serve dessert! Other families leave one day a week as an unscheduled, unstructured day and agree only to activities that are full of joy. Our family practice is similar to that of many others: Sundays begin with worship, end with a family movie, and usually include a nap somewhere in between.

Discuss ways for your whole family to cease working to rest in God. Build this habit for your child by including it as part of your family's weekly rhythm.

7. Journaling

The act of journaling is an opportunity to write down thoughts, feelings, and ideas as a means of reflection. Some Christians use journaling to write their prayers to God. Others use it to reflect on the events of a day to process thoughts and emotions with God's help. Still others use journaling to reflect on their thoughts and insights from the Scripture they read that day. For children who like to write, this practice may connect with their natural skills and help them identify God's work in their lives. Children can often express themselves better through writing than speaking, and this discipline gives them an opportunity to give words to their faith.

Art can also be a means by which a child journals their thoughts and has a conversation with the Lord. Drawings, sculptures, stories, poetry—each art form can help a child connect with God's Word, God's creation, and God Himself. Encourage them to use the gifts God has given them to connect with God. This builds confidence in those skills and connects them to the One who gave them those abilities.

8. Fasting

Though the practice of fasting is often associated with food, the heart of fasting is removing anything we might be addicted to or that takes on a role greater than God. Fasting provides an opportunity to take stock of what we're prioritizing in our lives and rearrange those things so that God always comes first.

Children can participate alongside their parents in fasting from certain foods (desserts, sweet drinks, or sugary snack foods) to instead enjoy food from the earth (fruits and vegetables) to remember God's creation. A family could fast from eating out for a period of time to donate the money they save to a ministry that provides food for those who go without. As children mature into adolescence, they can join you and others in fasting from food for a meal and filling that time with attention to God.[9]

If you find your child is giving too much attention to something particular in his life—taking selfies, playing video games, watching YouTube or a certain sports team—talk to him about how that might be distracting him from giving attention to more important things. Guide him through a period of fasting in which he gives that thing up. Talk with him along the way to help him recognize how he might be creating idols in his life.

This spiritual discipline can pay big dividends when children reach adulthood. Being self-aware enough to recognize when something is taking up too much time in our lives is humbling but necessary. Being disciplined enough to fast from those things to course correct is something that honors God and helps us focus on Christ. Give children this gift!

9. Gratitude

The final practice on the list is one that can be integrated with some of the others, but I wanted to make sure to give special attention to: expressing words of gratitude. In many households, our children have more than they need and yet do not have hearts of gratitude. Encourage children to practice thankfulness on a regular basis—to look for the things in their lives that are blessings and the joys of God's creation. Create a gratitude wall in their bedrooms or bathrooms on which they can write or draw things for which they're grateful. Provide a journal where they can write one thing a day that they can remember from that day that was good. During the month of November, create a thanksgiving list where each family member writes something they're thankful for each evening before dinner. Practice saying these things aloud to foster a spirit of gratitude in your kids.

The chart "Spiritual Practices for Children" provides a more detailed list of potential practices for each age of a child's development to encourage their continued growth as they mature in their relationship with God.

Building Holy Habits

These spiritual disciplines are a starting place for creating holy habits in the life of your child.[10] But do not feel that you must introduce all these in your child's life right away or at the same time. Instead, consider introducing your child to spiritual practices that might be a good fit for their personality, interests, and skills. As they mature, consider introducing a spiritual practice that might be a greater challenge for them. Participate together as a family so they aren't alone.

Talk about what is easy and difficult about spiritual practices. In these conversations you may hear your child describe how they are connecting to God.

For children who struggle with behavioral issues, emotional regulation, or anxiety, spiritual practices can come alongside other professional and medical treatment. Spiritual practices provide a space where children develop a relationship with God and create a secure attachment where they can feel safe, seen, soothed, and secure.[11]

Give your kids the gift of spiritual practices early in life so that just as they breathe air in and out each day, they breathe in and out the presence of God.

SPIRITUAL PRACTICES FOR CHILDREN

Age Range	Age-Appropriate Spiritual Practices
Establish God's Foundation: 0–12 Months (Infants)	• hear you pray, sing, and read Scripture
Demonstrate God's Love: 1–2 Years (Toddlers)	• repeat simple prayers • sing simple Bible songs • listen to Bible stories
Share God's Story: 3–4 Years (Preschoolers)	• recite simple prayers • sing simple Bible and memory-verse songs • select Bible stories to read • practice silence and solitude for thirty seconds
Engage God's Community: 5–6 Years (Kindergartners)	• say simple prayers in their own words • sing worship songs • practice silence and solitude for sixty seconds • give an offering when prompted • choose toys or other items to give away • be aware of church community practices like baptism and the Lord's Supper • join their family in sharing what they are thankful for

SPIRITUAL PRACTICES

Age Range	Age-Appropriate Spiritual Practices
Teach God's Truth: 7-8 Years (1st and 2nd Graders)	• pray in their own words in various settings • follow a basic prayer pattern • worship God through songs • practice silence and solitude for sixty seconds or longer • journal prayers or thoughts about God when prompted • give an offering from an allowance • choose to give up a gift or activity as an offering • help with service projects • explain Christian practices (baptism, Lord's Supper, offering, worship) in simple terms • fast from certain activities to spend time with Jesus • draw (on a gratitude wall or in a gratitude journal) that which they are thankful for
Reinforce God's Commands: 9-10 Years (3rd and 4th Graders)	• say aloud, write, or draw prayers without prompting • worship God through song and other activities • practice silence and solitude for a few minutes • journal prayers or thoughts about God as a regular practice • give an offering without prompting • identify potential ways to serve others or raise money for mission organizations or charitable causes • inquire about Christian practices that are unfamiliar or are from other Christian traditions • explain their participation in worship and other spiritual practices • fast from an activity they identify that is turning their attention away from Jesus • write one thing they are grateful for in a gratitude journal each day
Champion God's Calling: 11-12 Years (5th and 6th Graders)	• pray throughout the day, recognizing prayer as a relationship with God • practice silence and solitude for varying lengths of time • journal thoughts, reflections, emotions, and prayers • give a weekly offering or support a specific ministry/mission • identify ways to serve God with their talents and abilities • participate in the Lord's Supper, baptism, or other rituals of the faith • fast from specific foods for a length of time or join others in fasting from a meal (with a doctor's permission) • write notes of gratitude to friends, family members, and church leaders

Note: As a child progresses from age to age, they build upon the knowledge and skills from earlier stages.

TYING IT ALL TOGETHER

As Jesus walked alongside the Twelve, He taught them by example and instruction. They were with Him in the synagogue and witnessed His observance of the Sabbath. They heard Him teach about money and heard Him honor a widow who gave all she had to the Lord. They sang together, served together, and observed other religious practices together.

Amid this togetherness, the Gospels record numerous times that Jesus withdrew from the crowds and His disciples to pray, to spend time with God the Father through the power of God the Spirit. The Twelve had watched Jesus practice this habit and desired to learn from Him.

> One day Jesus was praying in a certain place. When he finished, one of his disciples said to him, "Lord, teach us to pray, just as John taught his disciples."
>
> He said to them, "When you pray, say:
>
> "'Father,
> hallowed be your name,
> your kingdom come.
> Give us each day our daily bread.
> Forgive us our sins, for we also forgive
> everyone who sins against us.
> And lead us not into temptation.'"
>
> LUKE 11:1-4

The disciples learned to pray, worship, serve, give, and practice other spiritual habits through observation, instruction, and participation. Every person who comes alongside a child can give them an opportunity to join them in their journey with Christ in these same ways.

PUTTING IT INTO PRACTICE

Questions for Reflection

1. Which spiritual practices are part of your daily life?

2. How has your child observed or participated with you in daily spiritual practices?

3. What spiritual practice could you introduce to your child or family this week?

4. What spiritual practice would best connect with your child's age, interests, or needs?

CHAPTER 6

Identity in Christ

My second-grade teacher, Mrs. DeYoung, handed out pieces of paper one day while instructing us to "draw a picture and write a description of what you want to be when you grow up." We all knew that we would eventually hang our papers on a bulletin board outside our classroom for everyone to see during the upcoming open house and parent-teacher conferences. My class was filled with those who dreamed of becoming doctors, teachers, professional athletes, and first responders. But my aspirations were higher. That morning I drew a picture of a woman with long, blonde hair and blue eyes standing behind a podium with a big circle in the front. On the lines below I recorded, "When I grow up, I want to be the first female president of the United States of America."

Identity formation is the process by which a child forms a unique view of herself in relationship to others. As she explores independence from parents and others, a child develops a sense of self. Our identities are shaped by our families, friends, peers, societies, cultures, and social groups. Regardless of what aspirations a child has for her future vocation, everyone who participates in the discipleship of a child should be guiding her toward finding her identity in Christ as she develops a personal relationship with God.

Considering the ways I have been encouraged since infancy, it is no surprise that I found my identity in Christ and my vocation in ministry. I regularly sang "special music" at church from the time I was two years old. I started turning the pages for the church organist while my parents were at choir practice when I was seven. I led my third-grade class in reciting Scripture on Promotion Sunday. I played piano for kids' worship when I was in junior high. My youth minister equipped me to lead a Bible study beginning during my freshman year of high school. I led congregational singing for our church as a high school junior. I participated in school and extracurricular activities throughout my childhood, but the identity that was formed within a Christian community as I traveled along the discipleship map is what set a trajectory for a life of service to God.

As a child reaches adolescence, he begins to wrestle with his identity. He begins to become aware of himself as separate from others and imagine his future self. Though he might articulate his search for identity in different ways, at the core he is struggling to answer three common questions: *Who am I? Where do I fit in? What is my purpose in the world?*[1]

Fortunately, Scripture answers these questions for us. We don't have to wait until our children reach adolescence to begin pointing them to the answers.

The First Question

Question: Who am I?
Answer: I am loved by God.

What was your nickname when you were a child? What did your parents call you? What did your friends call you? How did that shape what you thought about yourself? Maybe you had self-confidence because the nickname was encouraging. Perhaps you endured a nickname you'd have preferred not to have and to this day react negatively when someone uses it.

Now consider the names you use for the children in your life. What words do you commonly use to describe them? Do those words encourage their gifts and talents or the characteristics of God they exhibit?

From the time we enter the world, we create a story about our own lives. And that story shapes the things we tell ourselves about ourselves as we mature. Woven into this are the stories we hear others share about us and how we find ourselves fitting in, or not, in our family and social world.

As a child reaches puberty, you may observe them trying

to answer the question *Who am I?* Children may try a new activity, listen to a different genre of music, or choose to dress in a different style to help them answer this question. Regardless of which social group they've connected with, ethnic group they were born into, sport they play, or academic ability they possess, all children share the same identity under God.

The answer to the question *Who am I?* is this: *I am loved by God.*

Our holy, perfect, majestic, awesome, glorious God loves us. Yes, God is perfect and just and hates sin. But God loves us despite our sin. Yes, God desires us to be obedient to His commands, to walk in His ways. But God loves us even in our disobedience. Yes, God created humanity to love Him and love others. But God loved us first.

Paul writes a description of love to the church in Corinth. This well-known passage from 1 Corinthians 13 is often read as two people join their lives in marriage, but this passage is best read as a description of God's love for us that we might then extend to others. A colleague of mine recently suggested replacing the word *love* with the word *God* to understand the depth of God's love for us.

[God] is patient, [God] is kind. [God] does not envy, [God] does not boast, [God] is not proud. [God] does not dishonor others, [God] is not self-seeking, [God] is not easily angered, [God] keeps no record of wrongs. [God] does not delight in evil but rejoices with the truth. [God] always protects, always trusts, always hopes, always perseveres. [God] never fails.

I CORINTHIANS 13:4-8

How would a child's day-to-day life be different if every moment she were aware of the truth that God loves her? How would your life be different?[2]

A child can learn from infancy that God loves him by the words that are spoken over him in his crib and the songs that are sung over him as he is rocked to sleep. As he grows into a toddler and preschooler, repeat these words and guide him in saying and singing them out loud. When a child reaches his elementary-school years, continue to remind him of this truth. As you read Bible stories that point to God's love, remind your child that God loves him just like He loved Abraham, Moses, and Mary. When you remind your child with the words "I love you," add the truth that "God loves you even more."

As a child becomes aware of his or her sin and expresses feelings of guilt, remind them that God forgives their sin because of His great love for them. Encourage them to memorize and repeat verses like "God so loved the world" (John 3:16) and "We love because he first loved us" (1 John 4:19) and ". . . nor anything else in all creation, will be able to separate us from the love of God that is in Christ Jesus our Lord" (Romans 8:39). When a child experiences consequences for their sins, remind them that God corrects those He loves (Proverbs 3:11-12) and forgives all our sins (1 John 1:9).

One of my favorite things to do is to lead children in

singing songs of praise and adoration. A few years ago, a song became very popular on Christian radio and in congregational singing—"Good Good Father." The chorus contains these words:

> *You're a good, good Father.*
> *It's who You are. It's who You are. It's who You are.*
> *And I'm loved by You.*
> *It's who I am. It's who I am. It's who I am.*[3]

As we sing the words "And I'm loved by you," I lead children in using the "I love you" sign from American Sign Language. We make that sign in the air above our heads and hold it as we lower our hands and place them over our hearts. The message of this motion is *Who am I? I am loved by God.* My prayer as we sing is that, although the children might not yet fully understand the words or the signs they are using, this message will be imprinted on their hearts and minds.

The Second Question

Question: Where do I fit in?
Answer: I am a child of God, created in His image!

Think back to the first few days of a new school year and the terror of entering the lunchroom, searching for your place among the other students. Think about those times when you would look for a place to sit at a social gathering, at a sports practice, or during a church program. In that moment, you were seeking the answer to the question *Where do I fit in?*

It's a question children begin asking themselves long before they become teenagers, even if they don't know quite how to express it. Children look for others to accept them from infancy. Babies cry to receive attention. Being soothed teaches them that they have someone who sees them and can comfort them.[4] Toddlers successfully complete a task and look for someone to affirm them. Preschoolers grab a broom to help clean up because they want to please the adult nearby. Kindergartners show off their work or skill to anyone who will give them attention. A child's desire for acceptance transitions from adults to peers during their elementary-school years. Children look for others who have similar interests, skills, or abilities so they don't feel alone.

As a child seeks attention from others, help her recognize that the loving gaze of God is always upon her, for she is His child, created in His image. Each child is made in the image of God (Genesis 1:27). God blessed humanity with the gift of children (Genesis 1:28), who reflect Him (Genesis 9:6).

Our perception of a child is often skewed by awareness of his immature and inconsistent behavior. But if we step back for a moment, we can see that there is beauty in how each child interacts with the world. A child can remind us what it means to love unconditionally, forgive freely, and hope beyond reason. A child teaches us about honesty and joy and demonstrates the struggle of patience and self-control. I have often wondered if it is in the best moments of childhood, more than at any other time of life, that we come closest to reflecting God's image.

One way we can help a child come to this recognition is by catching her in the act of reflecting the image of God. Point out to her when she makes a good choice or demonstrates a characteristic of God. Name those things about her character that reflect the heart of God. Children love to hear words of praise and affirmation. How much better to affirm them with words like these: "You remind me of your heavenly Father when you are kind to your brother." "You look like Jesus when you care for your friend who is upset."

Another way we help children understand their connection to the Father is to connect them to all God's children. Connecting a child to the Christian community is an important spiritual habit to foster. The Christian community is vital to a child in helping him form his identity. Parents, encourage your child to have relationships with people of all ages within your community of faith. He needs spiritual big brothers and sisters, aunts and uncles, and grandparents—the family of God. Acceptance within this community can help shape his identity around a shared faith and relationship with God.

The Third Question

Question: What is my purpose in the world?
Answer: To love God and love others.

Your child is *becoming* . . . that's the whole purpose of their childhood. They are learning what they are becoming at school, on sports teams, in music practice, and through every person they interact with. If we are not intentional about guiding them toward what God has created them to be, then they could become something God doesn't desire for them. What are you intentionally—or unintentionally—encouraging your child into becoming? What are you hoping they become when they grow up? A superstar athlete, a successful business leader, a renowned physician, a music star? Does that becoming drown out God's intention for them?

If our goal is to raise disciples who look more and more like Christ, we must look at Jesus' actions and teaching. One day as Jesus was answering questions of the Pharisees and Sadducees, an expert in the law asked Him a question as a test.

> "Teacher, which is the greatest commandment in the Law?"
>
> Jesus replied: "'Love the Lord your God with all your heart and with all your soul and with all your mind.' This is the first and greatest commandment. And the second is like it: 'Love your neighbor as yourself.'"
>
> MATTHEW 22:36-39

Jesus' response to this question provides us the perfect response to questions such as "What am I supposed to do when I grow up?" or "Why do I exist?" or "What is my purpose in life?": Love God and love others. When a child is wrestling with a decision, we can use these two commands as their guiding principle.

The Importance of Service

We have already explored ways children can grow in their love of God through various spiritual practices. A final spiritual practice to introduce your child to is service.

One of the most proactive ways you can help your child find their purpose through loving God and loving others is by giving them opportunities to serve others. There's a universal misconception that children aren't ready or capable of serving in significant ways until they're older. The funny thing about that statement is that *older* is nebulous and follows us our whole lives. We can become convinced of this when we're children and never shed this idea that we're not good enough or ready enough or capable enough of serving in significant ways.

Young children are often barred from serving with the words *You're not big enough yet.* We can discourage a child's help because she won't do it as well or thoroughly as an adult. Instead of telling her no, exclaim, "Join me!" Instead of saying, "You're not ready yet," encourage: "Give it a try." Guide her as she does what she can to serve, and help reveal the unique talents God has bestowed on her to use for His Kingdom.

Instead of telling her no, exclaim, "Join me!" Instead of saying, "You're not ready yet," encourage: "Give it a try." Guide her as she does what she can to serve, and help reveal the unique talents God has bestowed on her to use for His Kingdom.

At every age a child can partner with parents or older siblings in service projects. If your church is collecting canned goods, take him to the grocery store. Let him pick out cans and physically take them off the shelf and put them on the conveyor belt. Have him take them to church and put them in the collection box. Let him use his hands and physically do the acts of service. If your church has a community service day, bring your child with you to help however he can. Find simple things—or not-so-simple things—that he can do to help. He can pick up sticks and throw them in a wheelbarrow or dust the lower shelves of a home. Don't limit what he is capable of. Children constantly cause us to marvel with their ability to go above and beyond when presented with a challenge. Besides which, you and others will probably find their joy at and enthusiasm for service an encouragement.

Sometimes children come up with ideas for service that seem impossible to accomplish. Maybe they've heard that there are children without clean water, or who frequently go without food. They'll say they want to fix that problem. Rather than telling them it's too big of a problem to overcome, encourage them to identify steps they could take or ministries they could partner with to help address those issues. One of the best bits of wisdom to help children of any age when facing overwhelming odds is this: The best way to eat an elephant is one bite at a time. Just take the first step. Help them discover one thing they could do to help, and then another, and then another, and so on until they've made headway toward accomplishing the lofty goal they have before them.

Last fall a fifth-grade girl approached me at church with a sign she had just made. She was going to set up a lemonade stand outside her house to raise money for a missionary overseas. I remember thinking of the many ways she was falling short. The sign wasn't very big. There were misspellings. I doubted that she could raise much money. There were so many ways she might not succeed. But then I realized that it was less about the few dollars she might raise and more about the fact that she was taking initiative and practicing service. And to her, a few dollars could spark something that could result in something much greater than the immediate need. She was participating in something way beyond the small community in which we lived. It was way beyond even this earth. She was participating in a Kingdom of Heaven activity with eternal ramifications.

As children mature from childhood into adolescence, root out the answer to the question *What is my purpose in the world?* within the assurance that they are children of God, created to do good works out of the unique talents they've been given, in service to His Kingdom. By using gifts for service, children gain confidence that they have God-given purposes in their lives. And *that*, ultimately, is what all of us desire throughout life as we endeavor to worship God and follow in the footsteps of Jesus.

JESUS' METHOD: EXPERIENTIAL LEARNING

Though Jesus had a home base (Capernaum), His purposeful travel provided opportunities for the disciples to watch Him put His message into practice. Yes, Jesus took the disciples on field trips. Some of these trips were to towns in Galilee and Judea, across the Sea of Galilee, into the area of the Gentiles, through the enemy area of Samaria, and ultimately to Jerusalem. Each event and location provided a new experience that connected Christ's message with the reality of life.

Their field trips were not just for observation but also opportunities for practice. As Jesus prepared the disciples to carry the message, He sent them out to practice sharing the Good News. Luke records two different occasions in which Jesus sent out the disciples. In Luke 9:1-6, Jesus sent out the Twelve with His message and power. The result is recorded in Luke 9:10-11.

When the apostles returned, they reported to Jesus what they had done. Then he took them with him and they withdrew by themselves to a town called Bethsaida, but the crowds learned about it and followed him. He welcomed them and spoke to them about the kingdom of God, and healed those who needed healing.

What happened next? The miracle of loaves and fishes. It appears that thousands of people had gathered because they had followed the Twelve from these towns to hear the Good News from Jesus.

Later Jesus sent out a larger group of seventy-two of His followers (Luke 10:1-24). These disciples who had witnessed miracles of Jesus and heard Jesus' teachings were given a specific message to share with others and returned afterward to discuss their experiences. This gave them the opportunity not only to practice sharing the Good News but also to reflect on their experiences. Jesus was preparing them for the time when He would no longer be with them, and they would be entrusted with His mission.

Did you go on class field trips during your childhood? I fondly remember the progression of elementary-school trips and the experiences of each one. Each year the trip was a little farther from our town and a bit more exciting. I remember climbing onto the school bus, exploring a new location, and later searching the gift shop for the perfect item to memorialize that trip. We learn not just by hearing information but also through our experiences with the information.

We can follow the pattern of Jesus. Children should be given opportunities to practice their faith. They can do this in a myriad of ways—retelling a Bible story at the dinner table, inviting a friend to attend church, or using their gifts to serve others. Throughout their lives children should be given directions, opportunities, and, most importantly, chances to discuss their experiences so they are prepared to try again.

IDENTITY STAGES OF BELIEF IN CHILDHOOD

Age Range	What a Child Should Believe about Themselves and Others
Establish God's Foundation: 0–12 Months (Infants)	• God loves me. • Mom loves me. • Dad loves me.
Demonstrate God's Love: 1–2 Years (Toddlers)	• God made me. • I can love others.
Share God's Story: 3–4 Years (Preschoolers)	• God made me special. • Jesus loves me. • I can help others. • I can share. • I can obey God.

Age Range	What a Child Should Believe about Themselves and Others
Engage God's Community: 5–6 Years (Kindergartners)	• God created me. • God loves me no matter what. • I can be kind to others. • I can obey parents and teachers. • I can learn about God. • I can do what God wants.
Teach God's Truth: 7–8 Years (1st and 2nd Graders)	• God loves everyone. • God forgives me. • I have sinned. • I can obey and follow God. • I can forgive others. • I can be a good friend. • I can invite friends to church. • Jesus died for sinners like me.
Reinforce God's Commands: 9–10 Years (3rd and 4th Graders)	• I am made in the image of God. • God loves everyone, even those who are not my friends. • God forgives everyone. • I am a sinner. • Jesus died for me. • I can choose to resist the temptation to sin. • God gave me special talents. • I can believe in and follow God. • I can tell my friends about God. • I can love everyone.
Champion God's Calling: 11–12 Years (5th and 6th Graders)	• I am a unique creation of God. • God loves everyone, the good and bad. • Everyone has sinned. • I can repent of my sins. • I can accept Jesus as my Lord and Savior. • God gave me talents to use to serve Him. • I can tell everyone about God. • I can love everyone, even those who are not kind to me. • I can study God's Word to learn more about Him. • I can be a good example to others.

Note: As a child progresses from age to age, they build upon the knowledge and skills from earlier stages.

Your Identity in Christ

My husband tells the story of a time when he and my step-daughter were in the car when she was three years old. It was a couple of weeks before Easter, and she was excited about the upcoming holiday. She was talking about the Easter Bunny and finding eggs and her favorite candies, and my husband took the opportunity to emphasize the importance of Easter. He explained the meaning of the death and resurrection of Christ in very simple terms for a three-year-old to understand. As he finished, there was a long pause before suddenly she said, "Daddy . . . I hear Jesus in your breathing when you're speaking."

To this day he says it's the best compliment he's ever been given.

Can your child hear Jesus in your breathing? If a child were asked to describe you . . . would she describe you as a follower of Jesus, a disciple? How would she identify you?

TYING IT ALL TOGETHER

As Jesus walked the roads teaching, healing, and pointing people toward the Kingdom of God, He didn't disciple just the Twelve but rather thousands of people. There were two sisters among the group of people who participated in His ministry.

As Jesus and his disciples were on their way, he came to a village where a woman named Martha opened her home to him. She had a sister called Mary, who sat at the Lord's feet listening to what he said. But Martha was distracted by all the preparations that had to be made. She came to him and asked, "Lord, don't you care that my sister has left me to do the work by myself? Tell her to help me!"

"Martha, Martha," the Lord answered, "you are worried and upset about many things, but few things are needed—or indeed only one. Mary has chosen what is better, and it will not be taken away from her."

LUKE 10:38-42

Martha, like any good hostess, cared about offering hospitality. But these preparations worried her to the point of distraction. Martha's identity was caught up in how she was perceived by her guests. Mary, on the other hand, chose to sit at Jesus' feet, where the disciples would sit. She knew her identity was in her relationship with Christ.

Jesus took the opportunity to redirect Martha, using the interaction as a teachable moment. He reset her priorities and emphasized the more important characteristic of seeking deeper knowledge of God and His Kingdom. It's not wrong to practice hospitality—in fact, most would probably agree that it's one of Martha's core spiritual gifts. But Jesus used that teachable moment to help her see that relationship with God is the ultimate purpose for which we were created.

PUTTING IT INTO PRACTICE
Questions for Reflection

1. When you were in elementary school, what did you want to be when you grew up? How was this dream encouraged or discouraged?

2. How were you encouraged to find an identity in Christ in your childhood, teen years, young adulthood, and today?

3. What do your children talk about becoming when they grow up? How are you supporting them in their dreams?

4. How are you encouraging your child to find their identity in Christ?

5. How might you remove any obstacles from your child placing their identity in being a child of God?

CHAPTER 7

Faith of Their Own

I remember the looks on their faces as they crossed the church lobby to talk with me one Sunday morning. With a mix of hope and uncertainty, Kevin and Susan asked me the question I've heard from parents many times: "Our son has been asking to get baptized. Do you think he is ready?"

In that moment I realized something that is true of many parents. There is so much you know about your child: his shoe size, teacher's name, favorite stuffed animal, and the kids he likes to hang out with. But what can sometimes elude you is how to assess his faith development. Specifically you don't know if your child is beginning to believe for himself the things you have been raising him to believe since infancy.

At what point does the discipleship map you have been guiding him on become the path that he has chosen to continue?

In the tradition in which I was raised, the act of baptism occurs at the time a child (or adult) arrives at a place of belief, confession, and repentance. In other traditions, the practice of confirmation is when a child articulates what she believes. Regardless of the Christian tradition in which you are raising your child, at some point in her discipleship journey she must choose the journey for herself. What does it mean for a child to make her faith her own?[1]

Examples from Scripture suggest knowledge of God and conviction of belief both define the time when a child reaches a faith of their own.

Biblical Examples of Children on the Discipleship Map

At the beginning of 1 Samuel, the prophet records the story of his birth and childhood. His mother, Hannah, prayed for a child, and in response to God answering her prayer, she gave Samuel to the Lord to serve alongside the priest Eli (1 Samuel 1:24-28). Based on the description "after he was weaned," Samuel's service would have happened during his early childhood, around age four.[2] Some years later, the Lord called to Samuel (1 Samuel 3:4-14). Samuel didn't recognize the voice of the Lord; instead, he believed Eli was calling him. His lack of awareness of God's voice is explained in 1 Samuel 3:7: "Now Samuel did not yet know the LORD: The word of the LORD had not yet been revealed to him."

The word translated "know" here is the Hebrew word יָדַע (*yāḏa'*). This word is used in the Old Testament to describe knowledge with understanding that comes from experience or perception. Since a young age, Samuel had worshiped the Lord at Shiloh (1 Samuel 1:24-28), where he was learning *about* God. But this encounter, which according to Jewish tradition happened at the age of twelve,[3] gave Samuel a direct experience *of* God.

In the New Testament, the apostle Paul wrote to a young Christian leader, Timothy, to encourage him in his God-given skills in leading a community of believers. In his encouragement, Paul reminds Timothy of how he came to believe in Jesus. Paul wrote,

> But as for you, continue in what you have learned
> and have become convinced of, because you know
> those from whom you learned it, and how from
> infancy you have known the Holy Scriptures, which
> are able to make you wise for salvation through faith
> in Christ Jesus. All Scripture is God-breathed and is
> useful for teaching, rebuking, correcting and training
> in righteousness, so that the servant of God may be
> thoroughly equipped for every good work.
>
> 2 TIMOTHY 3:14-17

Timothy's training for becoming a leader in the church began in infancy as he learned Scripture from his mother and grandmother (2 Timothy 1:5). Their teaching placed him on a discipleship journey, but Paul states that at some point along this journey, Timothy became convinced of the Scriptures. The word translated as "become convinced of" is a form of the Greek word πίστις (*pistis*) which is commonly translated "trust or faith."[4] Though Lois and Eunice raised Timothy to be a disciple, he had to become convinced that what they said was true. We don't know at what age Timothy became convinced, but from the time he was able to stand firm on his conviction, his faith was his own.

Timothy and Samuel are examples of those who learned about God in childhood and served him their entire lives. Their stories also point to the importance of guidance by parents and other adults along the discipleship map. Lois and Eunice taught Timothy the Scriptures. Eli led Samuel to worship God and guided him in hearing God's voice. Intentionality matters in raising disciples.

From Their Parents' Faith to a Faith of Their Own

What can parents do to help their children grow in their awareness of God and become convinced that Scripture is true?

I had struggled for years to articulate what I had discovered through my research, through observing hundreds of kids journey along the discipleship map, and through talking to adults about their own discipleship journeys. I could identify the changes I saw in a child's maturing faith. Sometimes maturity happened rapidly and at other times more slowly. What eluded me was the vocabulary or a structure that could help parents understand this point along the discipleship map . . . until a colleague introduced me to the research of French anthropologist Arnold van Gennep and his theory of liminality. You may not have heard his name before, but you probably know the phrase he coined: *rites of passage.*

---

liminality (lim-uh-nal-i-tee): a state of transition
that occurs between two stages of development,
between major life events, or during rites of passage[5]

In the early 1900s, van Gennep discovered there was a pattern to religious and cultural traditions from around the world. He summarized his findings in the book *The Rites of Passage.*[6] The phrase *rites of passage* has been used in conjunction with life-changing events: obtaining a driver's license, graduating from high school, getting married, buying a home, or giving birth. But what van Gennep discovered was that it wasn't just a single event—a rite—but rather three separate events that occurred in a common pattern. He labeled these three events *the rite of separation, the liminal rite,* and *the rite of incorporation,* respectively.

Before I explain why this helps us understand how a child develops a faith of their own as they journey along the discipleship map, let me explain van Gennep's basic theory. Take, for example, the rite of marriage. The moment one person gets down on one knee and the other person accepts their marriage proposal, the couple experiences the *rite of separation*. They have separated themselves from their old status (dating), but they aren't yet in their new status (married). The wedding ceremony is the *rite of incorporation*, when two adults pledge to live as one. They have entered a new status in their lives—that of Mr. and Mrs.

The time in between the proposal and the wedding— the engagement—is what van Gennep titled the *liminal rite*, or what some call *liminality*. It is during this time that the couple prepares for a new phase of life. This time is exciting because of new experiences in preparation for the new status. It is also difficult as the couple struggles with differences and perspectives that linger from the old states. Each person learns more about their future spouse and about themselves as they separate from their lives as single adults and prepare to live together in marriage.

Liminality is always a time of transition: No one is meant to remain in this stage indefinitely. Because it is a time of transition, liminality is a time for learning and transformation. It is a time for asking questions and seeking answers. During liminality there is a heightened interest in discovering new things, shedding the old, and preparing for what is to come. It sounds like the process Paul describes in 1 Corinthians 13:11—"When I was a child, I talked like a child, I thought like a child, I reasoned like a child. When I became a man, I put the ways of childhood behind me."

How do we help children put the immaturity of childhood behind, build upon the elementary teachings and become mature followers of Christ? Van Gennep's model applied to the discipleship map looks something like this:

- **Old status.** Parents and the community of believers introduce a child to faith. She hears the name of God and stories of the Bible from infancy (or early childhood). He attends church because his parents do. She participates alongside others in worship, prayer, and study.

- **Rite of separation.** A child actively demonstrates an interest in learning about God independent of his parents, community, or regular church participation. She begins asking questions about the reality of God and the truth of Scripture. He starts using his vocabulary of faith and demonstrates an interest in reading Scripture and discovering answers to his questions. She acknowledges her sins and identifies feelings of guilt.

- **Liminality.** A child begins to put into daily practice the vocabulary of his faith as he moves from concrete to abstract knowledge. He searches Scripture for answers to his questions and applies the Bible to his life. She asks difficult questions—"Why does God permit evil in the world?" or "Why did God allow my grandpa to die?" or even "Will we be naked in heaven?" He wonders if he can trust God. She may question why her friends participate in practices of faith differently or do not worship God. He can identify his sin but may not always be able to articulate why he sins. She is inconsistent in words and actions, but she is making efforts to love and obey God and love others.

- **Rite of incorporation.** A child articulates his faith in his own words and describes his relationship with God in personal terms. She confesses that Jesus is her Lord, acknowledges the impact of her sin, and desires to make a commitment to follow Christ for the rest of her life.

- **New status.** A child actively engages in an ongoing relationship with God. He believes that God loves him as he recognizes his sin and repents, coming up with a plan to not repeat his sin. She confesses her beliefs and faith in Christ, even when others around her—especially peers—do not agree with her. He begins to organize his daily life with thoughts and motivations dictated by the will and example of Jesus. She isn't perfect, but she demonstrates the fruit of the Spirit and a desire for growth in loving God and loving others.

RITES OF PASSAGE ON DISCIPLESHIP MAP

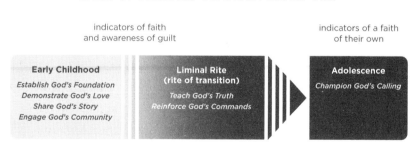

Different from someone experiencing what's described in the dramatic conversion stories of the New Testament (like Saul/Paul in Acts 9) or confession-and-baptism stories (like the Ethiopian eunuch in Acts 8), a child who learns about the Lord from infancy matures in faith through a combination of nurture and conviction. By using the rites-of-passage framework, we can better identify when a child is in that beautiful process of moving from a faith of his parents and community into a faith of his own.

This process may occur at any juncture along the discipleship map, as each child develops and matures uniquely.[7] But as I have come alongside kids in their discipleship, I believe that around ages seven to nine, as we focus on the discipleship directions Teach God's Truth and Reinforce God's Commands, children experience the rite of separation. As a child matures into a preteen, ages eleven to thirteen, when we concentrate on the discipleship direction Champion God's Calling, they experience the rite of incorporation. The years in between, the time of liminality, is so important for guiding them toward a faith of their own.

Our focus can be to become more active in our guidance when a child shows signs of liminality. Create safe spaces where a child can ask questions and dialogue about her doubts. Support and encourage her interest in spiritual conversations and practices. The writer of Hebrews states, "Faith is confidence in what we hope for and assurance about what we do not see" (Hebrews 11:1). The author then goes on to provide a list of individuals who acted on faith. If our goal for raising disciples is for a child to mature into an adult who will act on her faith in God, providing her with safe opportunities to question and even test that faith in childhood helps her faith grow.

As we walk alongside a child, remember that it is God who brings the growth. Some children will show readiness for spiritual maturity well before their peers. If this happens, encourage them to be open to the work of God in their lives and join them as they sprint ahead on the map. Others may take a longer path. Perhaps they need more time in preparation for the next leg of their journey. This could be due to distraction or lack of interest, or it might simply be that they just like to take their time at each stage. Though you might not be able to observe it, God may be helping establish a greater system of roots below the surface. Or, to use imagery from the parable of the sower (Luke 8), they may have rocks or thorns that need to be removed to allow for growth. Be patient, be faithful, be persistent—but also—trust God.

Whether in adolescence, young adulthood, or later in life, every person's faith will be tested. As James reminds us in his letter: "Consider it pure joy, my brothers and sisters, whenever you face trials of many kinds, because you know that the testing of your faith produces perseverance. Let perseverance finish its work so that you may be mature and complete, not lacking anything" (James 1:2-4). Our goal is to disciple children who will be "convinced of" what they have learned in childhood (2 Timothy 3:14) and can identify the voice of God so they can persevere in faith.

A Faith of My Own

It was April 18, 1982. I have a vivid memory of wearing my favorite purple dress in the stark sanctuary, which was punctuated by a bright green carpet that ran down the center aisle. I had nervously waited through the entire service—prayers, hymns, Communion, offering, choir offering, sermon— until we stood to sing the invitation hymn. As voices rose in the words of the hymn "Just as I Am," I walked to the front of the sanctuary. I had been preparing for this moment for about a week. (Actually, I had been preparing for that moment my entire life. In many ways I'm still preparing for that moment.)

I stood, holding the hand of Ellis Beeman, the senior minister at First Christian Church in Monmouth, Illinois, as he asked me to repeat after him the words "I believe that Jesus is the Christ, the Son of the living God." Moments later, I changed from my purple dress into a white baptismal robe, I stepped into the baptistery, and I was united with Christ in death and raised into new life through baptism.

Did I believe the words I spoke at the age of ten? Absolutely! I was fortunate to be raised by Christian parents and taught by loving volunteers. Have I grown into that confession over the past four decades? Most certainly! My belief that Jesus is the Christ has matured as I have continued in a lifelong journey of discipleship. But I remember that in the months preceding that initial confession I became convinced of the truth I had been learning from infancy. I can recall the voice of God convicting me of my sin and need for a Savior. I chose to make the faith of my parents and community a faith of my own.

TYING IT ALL TOGETHER

After a year of training the twelve disciples, teaching them His message and demonstrating His power, Jesus asked them a question to assess their learning and understanding.

> When Jesus came to the region of Caesarea Philippi, he asked his disciples, "Who do people say the Son of Man is?"
> They replied, "Some say John the Baptist; others say Elijah; and still others, Jeremiah or one of the prophets."
> "But what about you?" he asked. "Who do you say I am?"
> Simon Peter answered, "You are the Messiah, the Son of the living God."
> MATTHEW 16:13-16

This text is commonly called "the great confession." Although Peter was able to express the truth about Jesus' identity, when we follow His discipleship journey, we notice that Peter did not yet fully comprehend what he was saying. Just a little later, as recorded in Matthew 16, Jesus told the disciples He was going to be killed by the chief priests and other rulers. Peter exclaimed,

> "Never, Lord!" he said. "This shall never happen to you!"
> Jesus turned and said to Peter, "Get behind me, Satan! You are a stumbling block to me; you do not

have in mind the concerns of God, but merely human concerns."

MATTHEW 16:22-23

Peter knew how to respond to Jesus' question, but his understanding of his own response was incomplete.

A year later, Jesus gathered the disciples in the upper room for His final Passover meal. Later that evening Jesus told Peter that before the rooster crowed, Peter would deny knowing Jesus three times (Matthew 26:34-35). Peter boldly proclaimed that would never happen. Within hours, after Jesus was arrested, Peter stated three different times that he did not know Jesus (Matthew 26:69-75). Peter knew what he should do, but he lacked the courage or commitment to confess Christ that night.

But because of the events of that weekend and the days that followed, Peter's understanding of Jesus' identity and his commitment to his confession deepened, so that on the day of Pentecost, Peter preached a sermon to a great crowd that ended with this statement:

"Therefore let all Israel be assured of this: God has made this Jesus, whom you crucified, both Lord and Messiah."

ACTS 2:36

Peter's discipleship demonstrates that the journey with Christ is a process of growing in our understanding of what we believe and confess.

PUTTING IT INTO PRACTICE
Questions for Reflection

1. Consider your own discipleship journey.

   • From whom did you first learn about God?

   • How did they nurture and support your learning?

   • What questions did you have about God as you were maturing in your faith?

   • Can you identify your own journey through the rite of separation, liminality, and the rite of incorporation?

2. How does your faith tradition/denomination practice confession, baptism, and confirmation? How does that practice align with the idea of liminality?

3. In what ways can you support your children as they mature from the faith of their family and church community to their own faith?

Conclusion

I moved into my current home eight years ago. It was a new construction and the lot had to be cleared to construct the house. And so I planted some trees—two maples, one oak, and a flowering dogwood.

The local nursery gave me instructions on preparing the soil to plant the baby trees, to create a space where the trees could take root. They gave me instructions on loosening the established roots before planting and refilling the holes properly. They recommended a fertilizer to use periodically to help the trees grow and suggested ways to create space around the trunks for growth.

For eight years I have watched these four trees grow. I have fertilized. I have removed grass and replaced mulch. I have had branches pruned to allow for new growth. I have watched each spring as buds turn into leaves and marveled at how they hold on in the thunderstorms and winds that sweep across our area each year. I have enjoyed the growing shade they provide in summer and the beautiful colors of fall. And when I look at these trees, I am reminded of discipleship.

I am not the first to compare the growth of a tree to the process of discipleship—this idea is not original to me.[1] But I reference this image because it provides a picture of our lives following Jesus.

When I planted the saplings, they were small, fragile, and bore very few leaves from a small number of branches. But they were trees. They had roots, bark, branches, and leaves. They took in nutrients from the soil and the sun. What I can see surrounding my home now are trees that are more mature, yet have not reached their complete maturity. Each is a tree becoming a tree.

From the moment we were born, and even before this, in the womb, each of us was becoming. As Genesis 1 describes, every one of us is created, made in the image of God (Genesis 1:27). Though we are image bearers, we aren't fully mature when we enter the world. We aren't fully mature when we reach school age or puberty or adulthood or even retirement. Our entire lives are a process of "becoming" until we enter eternal life.

During different seasons, our processes of *becoming* might be focused on a particular aspect of life—becoming a student, friend, athlete, musician, artist, spouse, parent, or leader. These are branches of our lives in which we might focus our attention and energy. But the tree trunk is our identity as disciples of Christ, with our roots firmly placed in the good soil of the Word of God nourished by our ongoing relationship with God and within the community of faith.

As our faith grows, we are called to help in the growth of those around us.

There are a lot of ideas and practical application points contained within this book. The standard set is high and might feel impossible to meet. But you are not being asked to implement all of it within the next few days or weeks. Instead strive toward the integration of all these things in your own life and in the lives of children. The most important thing you can do as a parent is lead your child to follow Christ. The opportunity that God has placed before you with the children in your life is a high calling.

Parents, be present for your child and attentive to the Spirit leading you to specific opportunities and moments. Each year we become more distracted, and as your children get older, time flies faster and faster. You don't want to get to your child's senior year of high school and look back at all the moments you missed. So choose, right now, to be present for the moments God puts in front of you. Be present for the little moments—times around the dinner table, or times walking around the neighborhood, or times struggling over homework in the evening.

Here's the promise: You're not alone in this. Children's ministry leaders and volunteers, family members and the members of your Christian community—everyone has a role to play in raising disciples. If we're all guiding children along the discipleship map toward a faith of their own, the impact can extend into eternity.

You have Scripture to guide you. You have a community of faith to come alongside you. And you have the Holy Spirit, who will prompt you through those teachable moments and help illuminate your teaching. And remember, God loves your child even more than you do, and He will be with them every moment of every day for the rest of their life.

He is the One who unlocks the deeper truths of His Kingdom. God is the One who is present in the moments of your children's lives when you aren't around. And God will be the One to continue His work in their lives for years and years to come.

As I was writing this book, a friend asked, "What have you become more passionate about in the process of writing?" My answer is this: My desire is for every child to be guided from infancy to become a follower of Christ, so that he or she may never know a life without the knowledge of God and a relationship with Jesus. Or, more simply put—I'm more passionate than ever about raising disciples!

My prayer is that this book becomes a resource for you to disciple every child you know. May we follow in the footsteps of Christ, welcoming all children.

Jesus called the children to him and said, "Let the little children come to me, and do not hinder them, for the kingdom of God belongs to such as these. Truly I tell you, anyone who will not receive the kingdom of God like a little child will never enter it."

LUKE 18:16-17

Discussion Questions for Children's Ministry Leaders and Volunteers

Though this book was written for parents, you are a vital part of the discipleship journey. The information in this book can help you partner with parents in discipling children toward having an identity in Christ. The questions below are meant to help you reflect on the materials in each chapter through the lens of children's ministry.

Chapter 1: Becoming like Christ

1. Consider the activities that the children in your ministry, small group, or class participate in on a regular basis. How are these activities discipling these kids?

2. Reflect on your own childhood and how you were discipled during the first thirteen years of your life. In what ways do you want discipleship of children in your ministry to be similar? Different?

3. How does your own experience affect how you're discipling these children?

Chapter 2: The Discipleship Map

1. How do the programs you offer or lead correspond with the descriptions for each stage of discipleship?

2. How do the teaching materials (curriculum) you use help support this developmental approach to discipleship?

3. How can you better equip parents in your ministry for the various stages of the discipleship map?

Chapter 3: Learning and Studying God's Word

1. In what ways do you make the most of the opportunities given to you to teach children about God's Word?

2. What approach are you using to teach children age-appropriate Bible study methods?

3. What adjustments can you make to ensure that the curriculum you're using teaches Bible stories at age-appropriate levels?

4. What resources do you make available for volunteers to use—maps, atlases, concordances, timelines, et cetera?

5. What resources do you use to study the text you're teaching children? How can you enhance your personal study time prior to teaching kids?

Chapter 4: Vocabulary of Faith

1. What does your church or denomination use as their core belief statement(s)? Is there a version of this statement that uses language a child can understand?

2. How does the curriculum used support a child's learning the content of these statements?

3. How are you providing opportunities for children to ask questions about God?

4. What can you do to make sure you are asking open-ended questions every time you engage with children?

5. What resources do you make available to help volunteers teach kids vocabulary words or answer difficult questions?

Chapter 5: Spiritual Practices

1. What spiritual practices do you include in your regular weekly programming?

2. How do you incorporate times of silence and solitude or other quiet activities for children in your weekly programs?

3. If you use songs in your ministry, how do they help teach children about God? Do they contain an age-appropriate vocabulary of faith?

4. How could you train and empower your volunteers to incorporate various spiritual practices during times of worship, instruction, and small groups?

5. How are you encouraging relationships between the children in your ministry?

Chapter 6: Identity in Christ

1. When you were in elementary school, what did you want to be when you grew up? How was this dream encouraged or discouraged?

2. How were you encouraged to find your identity in Christ in your childhood, teen years, young adulthood, and today?

3. Who encouraged you toward serving in children's ministry? How has this service shaped your identity in Christ and your purpose in your faith community?

4. What opportunities are you giving children to practice their faith?

5. How are children encouraged to find their identity in Christ, and how does your ministry support them in this endeavor?

6. What might you do differently to better support older-elementary-aged children in developing a relationship with God?

Chapter 7: Faith of Their Own

1. Consider your own discipleship journey.

   - From whom did you first learn about God?

   - How did they nurture and support your learning?

   - What questions did you have about God as you were maturing in your faith?

   - Can you identify your own journey through the rite of separation, liminality, and the rite of incorporation?

2. How does your faith tradition/denomination practice confession, baptism, and confirmation? How does that practice align with the idea of liminality?

3. In what ways can you support the children in your ministry as they mature from having the faith of their family and church community to having their own faith?

Encouragement for Ministry Leaders

Make the most of the opportunities you have been given with every child God places in front of you. Your ministry is not programs and events but discipleship. Whether you are rocking babies in a nursery or teaching a small group of preteens, you are coming alongside a child in their discipleship. If you can be intentional about providing the foundational tools children need to be a follower of Christ, they'll carry those things with them the rest of their lives. If you can take advantage of teachable moments, they'll remember those lessons the rest of their lives. If you can model a life of a Christian, they'll mimic that the rest of their lives.

Resource List

Bible Dictionaries, Encyclopedias, and Atlases for Children's Use

Daryl J. Lucas, *The Baker Bible Dictionary for Kids* (Grand Rapids: Baker Book House, 1997)

The Complete Illustrated Children's Bible Atlas (Eugene, OR: Harvest House, 2017)

Deep Blue Kids Bible Dictionary (Nashville: Abingdon Press, 2017)

Melissa Hammer, *Faith Words for Kids: A Dictionary for Parents, Teachers, and Children* (Kansas City: Beacon Hill Press, 2011)

Landry R. Holmes and Judy H. Latham, eds., *Holman Illustrated Bible Dictionary for Kids* (Nashville: B&H, 2010)

Jean Fischer, *Kids' Bible Dictionary* (Ulrichsville, OH: Barbour, 2009)

Gina Detwiler, *The Ultimate Bible Character Guide* (Nashville: B&H Kids, 2020)

Bible Interpretation Resources for Parents and Ministry Leaders

John H. Walton and Kim E. Walton, *The Bible Story Handbook: A Resource for Teaching 175 Stories from the Bible* (Wheaton: Crossway, 2010)

Gordon D. Fee and Douglas Stuart, *How to Read the Bible for All Its Worth*, 4th ed. (Grand Rapids: Zondervan, 2014)

Resources for Discipleship of Children and Families

Kara Powell and Brad M. Griffin, *3 Big Questions That Change Every Teenager: Making the Most of Your Conversations and Connections* (Grand Rapids: Baker, 2021)

Ron Bruner and Dana Kennamer Pemberton, eds., *Along the Way: Conversations about Children and Faith* (Abilene, TX: Abilene Christian University Press, 2015)

Mark E. Moore and Megan Howerton, *Core 52 Family Edition: Build Kids' Bible Confidence in 10 Minutes a Day* (Colorado Springs: WaterBrook, 2022)

Justin Whitmel Earley, *Habits of the Household: Practicing the Story of God in Everyday Family Rhythms* (Grand Rapids: Zondervan Books, 2021)

Catherine Stonehouse, *Joining Children on the Spiritual Journey: Nurturing a Life of Faith* (Grand Rapids: Baker Books, 1998)

Michelle Anthony, *Spiritual Parenting: An Awakening for Today's Families* (Colorado Springs: David C Cook, 2010)

Diana Shiflett, *Spiritual Practices in Community: Drawing Groups into the Heart of God* (Downers Grove, IL: InterVarsity Press, 2018)

The Discipleship Map:
From Birth to Adolescence

Age Range	Discipleship Direction by Age Level
Establish God's Foundation: 0–12 Months (Infants)	Infants develop a sense of trust by forming a secure attachment with their caregivers, built upon constant care and genuine concern. Help establish an infant's attachment to God by laying this foundation of trust.
Demonstrate God's Love: 1–2 Years (Toddlers)	Toddlers perceive love through expressions such as hugs and kisses as well as through hearing the words "I love you." Demonstrate love through your words and actions. Tell them that God loves them too.
Share God's Story: 3–4 Years (Preschoolers)	Preschoolers shape their understanding of the world through the stories they hear, see, and experience. Involve them in reading the stories of the Bible and engage them in the rituals of worship, prayer, and service.
Engage God's Community: 5–6 Years (Kindergartners)	Kindergartners actively engage in learning through school and various activities. Encourage their involvement in exploring Bible stories and sharing prayers. Create an environment where they are comfortable asking questions and sharing their thoughts and opinions.
Teach God's Truth: 7–8 Years (1st and 2nd Graders)	First and second graders grasp the significance of God's stories by acknowledging the reality of God and the truth of God's Word. Encourage them to use their growing vocabulary of faith. Empower them to make decisions to follow Christ and obey God's commands.
Reinforce God's Commands: 9–10 Years (3rd and 4th Graders)	Third and fourth graders can connect the stories about God to their thoughts about God as they actively participate in the formation of their own beliefs. Guide them toward repentance as they are convicted about their sins and aware of their guilt. Lead them to accept God's forgiveness and grace.
Champion God's Calling: 11–12 Years (5th and 6th Graders)	Fifth and sixth graders express their identity through personal choices and peer relationships. Empower them in developing a personal relationship with God. Nurture their commitment to follow Christ. Foster their connections within a Christian community. Encourage them to recognize and utilize their God-given talents for His glory.

Age-Level Discipleship

Interspersed through the various chapters of *Raising Disciples* are charts that provide information pertaining to the discipleship map. This appendix takes that information and combines it for each age group for easy reference. My hope is that this is a helpful resource as you guide your child along their discipleship journey.

INFANTS (AGES 0–12 MONTHS)

Discipleship Direction	
Establish God's Foundation	Infants develop a sense of trust by forming a secure attachment with their caregivers, built upon constant care and genuine concern. Help establish an infant's attachment to God by laying this foundation of trust.
Development	
Cognitive and Behavioral	• learn large motor skills (rolling over, crawling, walking) • mimic the facial expressions of others • look at self in a mirror • respond to their name • begin to say simple words • are egocentric (do not comprehend a world that exists outside themselves)
Emotional, Social, and Moral	• recognize familiar faces • identify those who are unfamiliar as strangers • learn appropriate trust and distrust • thrive in a safe, consistent, and loving space • learn how to react to actions and express emotions • sense the emotions of their caregivers and the mood in their environment

God's Big Story	
Creation (Genesis 1–2)	• God loves me.
Fall (Genesis 3–11)	
Promise (Genesis 12–Malachi)	
Christ (Gospels)	• Jesus loves me.
Church (Acts, Epistles)	
New Creation (Revelation)	

Bible Knowledge and Skills	
Understanding of the Bible	• I love the Bible.
Knowledge of the Bible	• *simple concepts*: God, Bible, love
Training to Study the Bible	• identify a Bible

Faith Vocabulary	
God the Father	• God
God the Son	• Jesus
God the Holy Spirit	
Characteristics of God	• love
Faith Vocabulary	• Bible

Spiritual Practices	
Age-Appropriate Spiritual Practices	• hear you pray, sing, and read Scripture

Identity Stages of Belief	
What a Child Should Believe about Themselves and Others	• God loves me. • Mom loves me. • Dad loves me.

TODDLERS (AGES 1–2 YEARS)

Discipleship Direction	
Demonstrate God's Love	Toddlers perceive love through expressions such as hugs and kisses as well as through hearing the words "I love you." Demonstrate love through your words and actions. Tell them that God loves them too.

Development	
Cognitive and Behavioral	• master large motor skills through constant movement • practice fine motor skills • learn through their five senses and repeated activities • learn speech through repetition of hearing and saying words • begin to understand the meaning of words that are frequently repeated
Emotional, Social, and Moral	• imitate the actions of others • need a safe environment where they feel secure and loved • are appropriately fearful of strangers until familiarity is established • play alongside rather than with other children and learn appropriate behaviors • have a self-centered view of the world

God's Big Story	
Creation (Genesis 1–2)	• God created everything.
Fall (Genesis 3–11)	• God always loves us.
Promise (Genesis 12—Malachi)	• God loves everyone.
Christ (Gospels)	• Jesus is God's Son. • Jesus did great things.
Church (Acts, Epistles)	• God's people love me.
New Creation (Revelation)	• God made everything.

Bible Knowledge and Skills	
Understanding of the Bible	• The Bible is God's book.
Knowledge of the Bible	• Bible concepts: Jesus, creation
Training to Study the Bible	• identify a Bible • repeat three-word phrases/verses

Faith Vocabulary	
God the Father	• God
God the Son	• Jesus
God the Holy Spirit	
Characteristics of God	• love
Faith Vocabulary	• Bible
Spiritual Practices	
Age-Appropriate Spiritual Practices	• repeat simple prayers • sing simple Bible songs • listen to Bible stories
Identity Stages of Belief	
What a Child Should Believe about Themselves and Others	• God made me. • I can love others.

PRESCHOOLERS (AGES 3–4 YEARS)

Discipleship Direction	
Share God's Story	Preschoolers shape their understanding of the world through the stories they hear, see, and experience. Involve them in reading the stories of the Bible and engage them in the rituals of worship, prayer, and service.
Development	
Cognitive and Behavioral	• are extremely active with bursts of energy • have a short attention span (three to five minutes per activity) • have a rapidly growing vocabulary; use words appropriately without fully understanding their meaning • demonstrate curiosity through asking "Why?" repeatedly • can follow directions, but only one at a time • do not differentiate between make-believe and reality • learn about the world through concrete experiences
Emotional, Social, and Moral	• begin to understand right and wrong through behavior and correction • imitate the actions and words of those around them • transition from playing alone to playing with others • learn to share and to cooperate with others through taking turns • act according to emotions and feelings • need a loving environment with consistent routines and boundaries
God's Big Story	
Creation (Genesis 1–2)	• God created everything in seven days.
Fall (Genesis 3–11)	• Adam and Eve disobeyed God. • God saved Noah and the animals. • Rainbows are a sign of God's promise.
Promise (Genesis 12– Malachi)	• God keeps His promises, so follow God and obey His commands. • (Abraham, Isaac, Joseph, Moses, Joshua, Ruth, Hannah, David, Elijah, Esther, Daniel, Jonah)
Christ (Gospels)	• Jesus' birth • *miracles*: feeds five thousand, heals a paralyzed man, calms a storm • *parables*: lost sheep, Good Samaritan • Jesus' death, burial, and resurrection
Church (Acts, Epistles)	• Church is any place where we worship God and learn about Jesus with others who love God. • The church is God's family, who love me too.

New Creation (Revelation)	• Heaven is God's home.	
Bible Knowledge and Skills		
Understanding of the Bible	• The Bible is God's special book for us.	
Knowledge of the Bible	• simplified Bible stories	
Training to Study the Bible	• ask to be read to / read specific Bible stories • recite verses with five to seven words	
Faith Vocabulary		
God the Father	• Creator • Father	
God the Son	• God's Son	
God the Holy Spirit	• Holy Spirit	
Characteristics of God	• great • powerful	
Faith Vocabulary	• friend • helper	• obey • prayer
Spiritual Practices		
Age-Appropriate Spiritual Practices	• recite simple prayers • sing simple Bible and memory-verse songs • select Bible stories to read • practice silence and solitude for thirty seconds	
Identity Stages of Belief		
What a Child Should Believe about Themselves and Others	• God made me special. • Jesus loves me. • I can help others. • I can share. • I can obey God.	

KINDERGARTNERS (AGES 5-6 YEARS)

Discipleship Direction	
Engage God's Community	Kindergartners actively engage in learning through school and various activities. Encourage their involvement in exploring Bible stories and sharing prayers. Create an environment where they are comfortable asking questions and sharing their thoughts and opinions.

Development	
Cognitive and Behavioral	• are very active as they grow in their large and fine motor skills • have a growing attention span as they establish a consistent routine • mix their imagination and reality • have a growing vocabulary with a desire to understand new words as they learn to read
Emotional, Social, and Moral	• enjoy playing with other children • begin to relate to adults beyond their parents (teachers, coaches, family friends) • develop a sense of right and wrong based on rules and consequences • begin to see themselves as separate from others • are eager to please adults and desire praise for doing things well • need consistent and loving boundaries and Christlike behavior modeled • observe the behaviors of others and recognize inconsistency

God's Big Story	
Creation (Genesis 1-2)	• God created everything and it was good. • God created all people and it was very good.
Fall (Genesis 3-11)	• Adam and Eve sinned in the Garden of Eden. • God punished those who did not obey Him, but Noah obeyed God and was saved.
Promise (Genesis 12— Malachi)	• God loves us and has a plan for His people. • Abram answers God's call. • (story of Moses: birth, calling, plagues, Red Sea, Ten Commandments, wilderness, Promised Land)
Christ (Gospels)	• Jesus in the Temple at age twelve • *miracles*: blind man, deaf man, ten lepers • *parables*: wise/foolish builders • Triumphal Entry/Palm Sunday
Church (Acts, Epistles)	• Peter and John heal a lame man. • Paul, Silas, and the Philippian jailer • *Epistles*: fruit of the Spirit

New Creation (Revelation)	• Heaven is a perfect place.

Bible Knowledge and Skills

Understanding of the Bible	• The Bible tells us God's story.
Knowledge of the Bible	• Bible stories and characters • *Two sections:* Old and New Testaments • simple application of Bible to life
Training to Study the Bible	• read from a Bible storybook with assistance • recite verses in simple sentences • identify key Bible stories and characters

Faith Vocabulary

God the Father	• God Almighty
God the Son	• Savior
God the Holy Spirit	• Spirit of God
Characteristics of God	• good • kind • mighty • one and only God
Faith Vocabulary	• commandment • gentleness • goodness • kindness • patience • trust • worship

Spiritual Practices

Age-Appropriate Spiritual Practices	• say simple prayers in their own words • sing worship songs • practice silence and solitude for sixty seconds • give an offering when prompted • choose toys or other items to give away • be aware of church community practices like baptism and the Lord's Supper • join their family in sharing what they are thankful for

Identity Stages of Belief

What a Child Should Believe about Themselves and Others	• God created me. • God loves me no matter what. • I can be kind to others. • I can obey parents and teachers. • I can learn about God. • I can do what God wants.

1ST AND 2ND GRADERS (AGES 7–8 YEARS)

Discipleship Direction	
Teach God's Truth	First and second graders grasp the significance of God's stories by acknowledging the reality of God and the truth of God's Word. Encourage them to use their growing vocabulary of faith. Empower them to make decisions to follow Christ and obey God's commands.

Development	
Cognitive and Behavioral	• are active, talkative, imaginative, and eager to learn new information • have a continually expanding vocabulary as they learn to read and write • have a growing understanding of the world through concrete experiences • begin to separate their understanding of what is real and what is make-believe
Emotional, Social, and Moral	• like to play with others and be involved in groups • seek attention from teachers and other adults; imitate their behaviors • develop an understanding of and attitude toward self and others • are emotionally immature; act based on emotions • develop a sense of right and wrong based on consequences • need patient, caring adults who listen to questions and provide a safe environment

God's Big Story	
Creation (Genesis 1–2)	• God created Adam and Eve. • The Garden of Eden was perfect.
Fall (Genesis 3–11)	• Adam and Eve were tempted into sin. • God loves us even when we disobey. • People built the tower of Babel to glorify themselves, not God.
Promise (Genesis 12—Malachi)	• The history of the people of God in the Old Testament: Abram → Isaac → Jacob → Joseph → Moses → Joshua → Judges → Saul → David → Solomon → Daniel → Esther
Christ (Gospels)	• birth of John the Baptist • Jesus resists temptation. • Jesus calls the disciples to follow Him. • *miracles*: catch of fish, walking on water, official's son, widow's son • *parables*: sower/soils • upper room/Last Supper • great commission and Ascension

Church (Acts, Epistles)	• The Holy Spirit comes on Pentecost. • birth of the church • Saul's conversion • Peter in prison • Paul's missionary journeys • *Epistles*: body of Christ
New Creation (Revelation)	• Heaven is where we will live with God forever. • Christ will return to take us to heaven.

Bible Knowledge and Skills

Understanding of the Bible	• The Bible is God's Word. • God's Word is true.
Knowledge of the Bible	• Bible stories with more details • "God's big story" outline • identification of stories in the Old Testament or New Testament • Bible stories and characters related to their own life and experiences
Training to Study the Bible	• read Bible stories on their own (Bible storybook or NIrV, NCB) • recite core Bible verses • locate Bible verses with minimal help • list the books of the Bible in order

Faith Vocabulary

God the Father	• Everlasting God	• God Most High	
God the Son	• Christ	• miracle worker	
God the Holy Spirit	• Helper		
Characteristics of God	• all-powerful • compassionate • faithful	• glorious • perfect	
Faith Vocabulary	• angels • baptism • believe • cross • crucifixion • devil	• faithfulness • forgive • heaven • joy • miracle	• peace • resurrection • self-control • sin • truth

Spiritual Practices	
Age-Appropriate Spiritual Practices	• pray in their own words in various settings • follow a basic prayer pattern • worship God through songs • practice silence and solitude for sixty seconds or longer • journal prayers or thoughts about God when prompted • give an offering from an allowance • choose to give up a gift or activity as an offering • help with service projects • explain Christian practices (baptism, Lord's Supper, offering, worship) in simple terms • fast from certain activities to spend time with Jesus • draw (on a gratitude wall or in a gratitude journal) that which they are thankful for
Identity Stages of Belief	
What a Child Should Believe about Themselves and Others	• God loves everyone. • God forgives me. • I have sinned. • I can obey and follow God. • I can forgive others. • I can be a good friend. • I can invite friends to church. • Jesus died for sinners like me.

3RD AND 4TH GRADERS (AGES 9-10 YEARS)

Discipleship Direction	
Reinforce God's Commands	Third and fourth graders can connect the stories about God to their thoughts about God as they actively participate in the formation of their own beliefs. Guide them toward repentance as they are convicted about their sins and aware of their feelings of guilt. Lead them to accept God's forgiveness and grace.
Development	
Cognitive and Behavioral	• learn through active engagement in concrete experiences • begin to demonstrate strength in certain skills and pursue opportunities related to their strengths • develop speed and accuracy in skills through repetition • are frustrated by activities that are beyond their abilities • begin to understand abstract concepts but are more comfortable with concrete experiences, stories, or examples • are able to understand past, present, and future and can place events in order • make connections between information they are learning and their own experience
Emotional, Social, and Moral	• desire to be recognized by adults and assist them in their work • want to be accepted and belong to a group of peers, usually of the same gender • believe what is right and wrong is based on adherence to rules or what is fair • become less dependent upon their parents and other adults • are unable to regulate emotions (which may be expressed in anger or teasing) • need a patient, caring adult who encourages their skills and provides assistance in areas that are beyond their ability level
God's Big Story	
Creation (Genesis 1-2)	• In the beginning God created the world. • God is eternal. • God created us to be in relationship with Him.
Fall (Genesis 3-11)	• Sin entered the world through Adam and Eve's disobedience. • Sin separates us from God's presence.

Promise (Genesis 12— Malachi)	• *Covenant*: God establishes His people through Abram. • *Exodus/Tabernacle*: God leads His people. • *Judges*: People sin, repent, and are saved. • *Kings/Temple*: The people of God desire to be like other nations. • *Prophets/Exile*: Prophets call people to remember God's commands and repent. They also point toward Jesus.
Christ (Gospels)	• *baptism*: Jesus is the Messiah, the Son of God, who takes away our sin. • *miracles*: Jairus's daughter, bleeding woman, Transfiguration • *parables*: lost sons (prodigals), talents, rich man and Lazarus • *teaching*: Sermon on the Mount • Judas's betrayal, arrest/Gethsemane, Peter's denial and restoration
Church (Acts, Epistles)	• Peter's sermon on Pentecost • Philip and the Ethiopian • *Epistles*: lessons from James and Peter
New Creation (Revelation)	• description of new heaven and new earth
Bible Knowledge and Skills	
Understanding of the Bible	• The Bible is God's revelation to us.
Knowledge of the Bible	• Bible stories in cultural context • new-to-them Bible stories and characters • Bible chronology • Scripture applied to life, including problems and struggles
Training to Study the Bible	• read the Bible daily with minimal prompting • recite Bible verses • locate Bible verses on their own • use Bible dictionary and map • ask questions about Bible stories
Faith Vocabulary	
God the Father	• Abba • Alpha and Omega
God the Son	• God and man • King • Lord/Master
God the Holy Spirit	• Guide • Teacher

Characteristics of God	• all-knowing • everlasting • holy	• merciful • righteous • unchanging
Faith Vocabulary	• confess • disciple • eternal life • faith • glorify • mercy	• praise • prophecy • repent • sacrifice • salvation • saved

Spiritual Practices

Age-Appropriate Spiritual Practices	• say aloud, write, or draw prayers without prompting • worship God through song and other activities • practice silence and solitude for a few minutes • journal prayers or thoughts about God as a regular practice • give an offering without prompting • identify potential ways to serve others or raise money for mission organizations or charitable causes • inquire about Christian practices that are unfamiliar or are from other Christian traditions • explain their participation in worship and other spiritual practices • fast from an activity they identify that is turning their attention away from Jesus • write one thing they are grateful for in a gratitude journal each day

Identity Stages of Belief

What a Child Should Believe about Themselves and Others	• I am made in the image of God. • God loves everyone, even those who are not my friends. • God forgives everyone. • I am a sinner. • Jesus died for me. • I can choose to resist the temptation to sin. • God gave me special talents. • I can believe in and follow God. • I can tell my friends about God. • I can love everyone.

5TH AND 6TH GRADERS (AGES 11–12 YEARS)

Discipleship Direction	
Champion God's Calling	Fifth and sixth graders express their identity through personal choices and peer relationships. Empower them in developing a personal relationship with God. Nurture their commitment to follow Christ. Foster their connections within a Christian community. Encourage them to recognize and utilize their God-given talents for His glory.
Development	
Cognitive and Behavioral	• demonstrate individual preferences for learning environments ranging from loud, energetic groups to quiet, reflective spaces • desire to gain knowledge through discussion of topics of interest • like competition when they are successful and can demonstrate their skills • display abstract thinking by understanding concepts not tied to physical objects • apply deductive reasoning to anticipate outcomes • remain reliant on concrete experiences for understanding • need challenges and opportunities to demonstrate developing skills • recognize differences between their thoughts and beliefs and those of others
Emotional, Social, and Moral	• desire independence but also acceptance by peers • identify heroes and those they desire to model • believe that right and wrong are based on rules, laws, and obedience • desire to assist in creating the boundaries and consequences; need a reason to follow rules • are influenced in attitude toward self by acquisition of skills and acceptance by others
Emotional, Social, and Moral	• develop attitudes toward social groups and institutions (school, church, organizations) • need firm, loving boundaries to provide a secure environment where they are supported and encouraged while simultaneously held accountable for actions
God's Big Story	
Creation (Genesis 1–2)	• God created a world that demonstrates His wonderful design and order. • God created all people in His image. • There was a perfect relationship between Adam, Eve, and God in the Garden.

Fall (Genesis 3–11)	• Cain killed his brother Abel. • God held Cain accountable for his attitude and his actions. • God gave grace to Noah while still judging the sin in the world.
Promise (Genesis 12–Malachi)	• Connecting the Old Testament to the New Testament: Both include covenant, law, sacrifice, sin, repentance, restoration, and prophecy.
Christ (Gospels)	• Jesus is fully God and fully man. • baptism: God the Father, Son, and Spirit • miracles: demon-possessed man, raising of Lazarus • parables: unmerciful servant, worker and wages, rich fool, wedding feast • teaching: cost of discipleship, woman at the well, Peter's confession • Jesus washes the disciples' feet. • Jesus cleanses the Temple. • road to Emmaus
Church (Acts, Epistles)	• stoning of Stephen • Paul in Athens • Paul's arrest, shipwreck, imprisonment • Epistles: teaching from Paul's letters
New Creation (Revelation)	• hell and judgment • tree of life in heaven

Bible Knowledge and Skills

Understanding of the Bible	• The Bible guides me in my developing relationship with God.
Knowledge of the Bible	• Bible stories with more details, including historical, cultural, and literary context • genres of Scripture • expand study of Scripture to include Psalms, Prophets, and Epistles
Training to Study the Bible	• read the Bible on their own (NIV, NLT) • recite sections of Bible passages • use Bible concordance • reference the Bible for answers to their questions

Faith Vocabulary

God the Father	• I AM (YHWH)	
God the Son	• Emmanuel • human and divine	• Messiah • Prince of Peace
God the Holy Spirit	• Advocate • Comforter • Counselor	

Characteristics of God	• all-present • eternal • gracious • infinite • Judge	• just • Shepherd • triune/Trinity • wise
Faith Vocabulary	• atonement • covenant • demons • gospel • grace • hell • imago Dei	• judgment • justification • pardon • revelation • soul • wrath

Spiritual Practices

Age-Appropriate Spiritual Practices	• pray throughout the day, recognizing prayer as a relationship with God • practice silence and solitude for varying lengths of time • journal thoughts, reflections, emotions, and prayers • give a weekly offering or support a specific ministry/mission • identify ways to serve God with their talents and abilities • participate in the Lord's Supper, baptism, or other rituals of the faith • fast from specific foods for a length of time or join others in fasting from a meal (with a doctor's permission) • write notes of gratitude to friends, family members, and church leaders

Identity Stages of Belief

What a Child Should Believe about Themselves and Others	• I am a unique creation of God. • God loves everyone, the good and bad. • Everyone has sinned. • I can repent of my sins. • I can accept Jesus as my Lord and Savior. • God gave me talents to use to serve Him. • I can tell everyone about God. • I can love everyone, even those who are not kind to me. • I can study God's Word to learn more about Him. • I can be a good example to others.

Acknowledgments

To the communities of faith in Newark, Ohio; Westerville, Ohio; and Monmouth, Illinois—I am forever grateful for those who came alongside my parents from the time I was just a few weeks old to help raise me as a disciple of Christ. Your love of Jesus and love for me has had a more profound impact than you will ever know.

To "my kids" from New Philadelphia, Ohio; Decatur, Illinois; and Sylvania, Ohio—I thank my God every time I remember you, and I continue to pray that you are following Jesus and raising your kids to be disciples. Special thanks to the families in those communities of faith who welcomed me as part of their family.

To those who have been my teachers along my academic journey—your love for God and commitment to serving the church have shaped me. Special thanks to the late Dr. Eleanor Daniel for passing on a legacy of discipling others through teaching, training, and writing.

To my colleagues at Ozark Christian College and Emmanuel Christian Seminary—I love being your co-laborer in the gospel and in training men and women to serve the Kingdom.

To my students, especially my KidMin majors—I am excited to bear witness to your lives and ministries as you go forth and raise disciples. Thanks for helping me work on these ideas among you and for listening to me say over and over . . . children are not the future of the church—they are the church now!

To the team at NavPress and Tyndale that brought this book into the world—thank you for joining me on this journey to equip others to raise disciples.

To Miriam—thanks for your years of friendship and encouragement that I had something worthy to share through writing.

To my brothers, Doug and Kyle—I am so glad God gave me the two of you for this lifelong journey. I'm your biggest fan. Thanks to your wives, Noi and Monica, for loving you well and joining the Welch clan. And to my nephew, Jake, and niece, Allie—I love watching your mom and dad raising you to love Jesus! I can't wait to see what God does through you two!

To Lorelai—thanks for letting me be your stepmom. I am so proud of how I see Christ shine in your life. My constant prayer is that you will know how much I love you, your dad loves you, but most of all, that Jesus loves you.

To my husband, Chris—as I conclude the three-year journey of writing this book, I am overwhelmed with gratitude for your unwavering love and support. Your role in bringing this book into fruition cannot be overstated. Thank you for being my companion in listening to my ideas, in reading every semicolon, and in bringing thoughts and ideas to the page. It's not lost on me that we met because we share a passion for raising disciples. I am excited for the future we share in nurturing Lorelai, empowering parents, and collaborating in ministry. Thanks for being my biggest champion. I love you!

To God—may the words on these pages honor You above all else and help bring others to know and love You.

Notes

CHAPTER 1 | BECOMING LIKE CHRIST

1. First thirteen years of life: ages zero to twelve.
2. Many resources describe the growth of a child from infancy through adolescence, such as John W. Santrock, *Life-Span Development*, 19th ed. (New York: McGraw Hill, 2023).
3. See Jean Piaget and Bärbel Inhelder, *The Psychology of the Child*, trans. Helen Weaver (New York: Basic Books, 1969).
4. See Erik H. Erikson, *Childhood and Society*, 2nd ed. (New York: W. W. Norton, 1993).
5. See Lawrence Kohlberg, *Essays on Moral Development*, vol. 1, *The Philosophy of Moral Development: Moral Stages and the Idea of Justice* (San Francisco: Harper and Row, 1981).
6. See appendix D for a chart on childhood development in each of these categories.
7. For an overview of childhood development through the lens of a Christian worldview, please see Catherine Stonehouse, *Joining Children on the Spiritual Journey: Nurturing a Life of Faith* (Grand Rapids: Baker, 1998).
8. See Search Institute (searchinstitute.org) for information on the developmental assets every child needs.
9. For research on the importance of childhood discipleship, please see the following works: George Barna, *Transforming Children into Spiritual Champions: Why Children Should Be Your Church's #1 Priority* (Ventura, CA: Regal, 2003); Kara E. Powell and Chap Clark, *Sticky Faith: Everyday Ideas to Build Lasting Faith in Your Kids* (Grand Rapids: Zondervan, 2011); Valerie Bell et al., *Resilient: Child Discipleship and the Fearless Future of the Church* (Marceline, MO: Walsworth, 2020).

10. Darrell L. Bock, *Luke*, Baker Exegetical Commentary on the New Testament, Volume 1—1:1–9:50 (Grand Rapids: Baker, 1994), 264.
11. See the footnote for this verse in the NIV.
12. Erikson, *Childhood and Society*, 261–63.

CHAPTER 2 | THE DISCIPLESHIP MAP

1. The faith research of James W. Fowler (*Stages of Faith: The Psychology of Human Development and the Quest for Meaning* [San Francisco: Harper and Row, 1981]) and insights of spiritual development from John H. Westerhoff III (*Will Our Children Have Faith?*, 3rd. ed. [Harrisburg, PA: Morehouse, 2012]) have also informed this discipleship map.
2. See Curt Thompson, "Attachment: The Connections of Life," in *Anatomy of the Soul: Surprising Connections between Neuroscience and Spiritual Practices That Can Transform Your Life and Relationships* (Carol Stream, IL: Tyndale, 2010), 109–34.
3. John W. Santrock, *A Topical Approach to Life-Span Development*, 10th ed. (New York: McGraw Hill, 2020), 190–91.

CHAPTER 3 | LEARNING AND STUDYING GOD'S WORD

1. Though it is ideal for every person to begin to learn the Word of God in childhood, it is never too late to begin to dive into God's Word!
2. The Bible is approximately 775,000 words when translated into English. An adult who reads at the average speed of two hundred words per minute would take about sixty-five hours to read the whole Bible. For infographics on Bible reading time, see "Infographic: You Have More Time for Bible Reading than You Think," Crossway, November 19, 2018, https://www .crossway.org/articles/infographic-you-can-read-more-of-the-bible-than -you-think.
3. A great resource for parents and teachers to use in teaching children stories from the Bible is John H. Walton and Kim E. Walton, *The Bible Story Handbook: A Resource for Teaching 175 Stories from the Bible* (Wheaton, IL: Crossway, 2010).

CHAPTER 4 | VOCABULARY OF FAITH

1. Paul Bloom, *How Children Learn the Meanings of Words* (Cambridge, MA: MIT Press, 2002), 25.
2. See resources such as Melissa Hammer, *Faith Words for Kids: A Dictionary for Parents, Teachers, and Children* (Kansas City: Beacon Hill Press, 2011) and the list of Bible dictionaries provided in appendix B for additional guidance on teaching these important words.

3. The questions for this assignment were inspired by James W. Fowler, *Stages of Faith: The Psychology of Human Development and the Quest for Meaning* (San Francisco: Harper and Row, 1981) and the questions he asked his research subjects in understanding faith formation.

CHAPTER 5 | SPIRITUAL PRACTICES

1. Whether or not you were encouraged to develop spiritual practices and holy habits in your childhood, God is always at work in our lives and can guide us in forming a relationship with Him, no matter our age or circumstance.
2. For those interested in further studying the power of music in the discipleship of children, please see Yancy Wideman Richmond, *Sweet Sound: The Power of Discipling Kids in Worship* (Murfreesboro, TN: Yancy Ministries, 2021).
3. Geoffrey W. Bromiley, trans., *Theological Dictionary of the New Testament*, abridged in one volume, ed. Gerhard Kittel and Gerhard Friedrich (Grand Rapids: Eerdmans, 1985), 397–402.
4. A resource for understanding the importance of the relationship between teacher and student can be found in the research of Charles Bingham and Alexander M. Sidorkin, eds., *No Education without Relation* (New York: Peter Lang, 2004).
5. The Search Institute in Minneapolis has identified forty developmental assets that support and strengthen children. Their research can be found at https://searchinstitute.org/resources-hub/developmental-assets-framework.
6. See Blue Letter Bible, s.v. "*rapa*," accessed May 17, 2024, https://www.blueletterbible.org/lexicon/h7503/niv/wlc/0-1; Allen P. Ross, *A Commentary on the Psalms: Volume 2 (42–89)* (Grand Rapids: Kregel, 2013), 104.
7. Ruth Haley Barton, *Invitation to Solitude and Silence: Experiencing God's Transforming Presence*, expanded ed. (Downers Grove, IL: InterVarsity Press, 2010), 34–35.
8. For a further explanation of this spiritual practice as well as other practices you can do as a family, please see Diana Shiflett, *Spiritual Practices in Community: Drawing Groups into the Heart of God* (Downers Grove, IL: InterVarsity Press, 2018), 30–32.
9. Inviting your child to fast from a meal or for longer should be done in conjunction with medical advice and what is best for your child's nutritional needs.
10. See Justin Whitmel Earley, *Habits of the Household: Practicing the Story of God in Everyday Family Rhythms* (Grand Rapids: Zondervan, 2021) for additional ideas and instructions on spiritual practices for families.

11. See Curt Thompson, "Attachment: The Connections of Life," in *Anatomy of the Soul: Surprising Connections between Neuroscience and Spiritual Practices That Can Transform Your Life and Relationships* (Carol Stream, IL: Tyndale, 2010), 109–34.

CHAPTER 6 | IDENTITY IN CHRIST

1. These three questions are modified slightly from the three questions addressed by Kara Powell and Brad M. Griffin, *3 Big Questions That Change Every Teenager: Making the Most of Your Conversations and Connections* (Grand Rapids: Baker, 2021).
2. I recommend James Bryan Smith, *The Good and Beautiful God: Falling in Love with the God Jesus Knows* (Downers Grove, IL: IVP, 2009) for those who would like to better understand the nature of God's love.
3. Lyrics excerpted from "Good Good Father," written by Anthony Brown and Pat Barrett (Capitol CMG Paragon, 2014) and popularized by Chris Tomlin.
4. See Curt Thompson, "Attachment: The Connections of Life," in *Anatomy of the Soul: Surprising Connections between Neuroscience and Spiritual Practices That Can Transform Your Life and Relationships* (Carol Stream, IL: Tyndale, 2010), 109–34.

CHAPTER 7 | FAITH OF THEIR OWN

1. See the four stages of faith (experienced faith, affiliative faith, searching faith, and owned faith) from John H. Westerhoff III, *Will Our Children Have Faith?*, 3rd ed. (Harrisburg, PA: Morehouse, 2012), 90–91.
2. According to Jewish literature of this time (2 Maccabees), women would nurse children through age three or later. This was most likely due to lack of clean water and to provide nutrition to infants and toddlers. David Toshio Tsumura, *The First Book of Samuel*, New International Commentary on the Old Testament (Grand Rapids: Eerdmans, 2007), 128–29.
3. Robert D. Bergen, *1, 2 Samuel*, The New American Commentary, vol. 7 (Nashville: B&H, 1996), 86.
4. Geoffrey W. Bromiley, trans. *Theological Dictionary of the New Testament*, abridged in one volume, ed. Gerhard Kittel and Gerhard Friedrich (Grand Rapids: Eerdmans, 1985), 853.
5. This definition is informed by the research of Arnold van Gennep, *The Rites of Passage*, 2nd ed., trans. Monika B. Vizedom and Gabrielle L. Caffee (Chicago: University of Chicago Press, 2019) and Victor Turner, *The Ritual Process: Structure and Anti-Structure* (New Brunswick, NJ: Aldine Transaction, 1969).

6. Arnold van Gennep, *Les rites de passage* (France, 1909).
7. Different faith traditions may encourage specific activities for children at different stages of this process. Some traditions believe that a child should publicly confess Christ and submit to the act of baptism at an age of accountability. According to the rites of passage, baptism is their rite of incorporation. Other traditions may encourage a public confession as the rite of separation and baptism as the rite of incorporation. Still others might see a connection between the practice of confirmation and the rite of incorporation. Regardless of the specific tradition in which a child is being reared to believe in and follow Jesus, understanding van Gennep's rites of passage helps us come alongside children during the liminal stage so that they might choose the new status in Christ.

CONCLUSION
1. John H. Westerhoff III, *Will Our Children Have Faith?*, 3rd ed. (Harrisburg, PA: Morehouse, 2012), 90–91.